TURNING TRAGEDY INTO VICTORY

Lessons Learned from Cops
Who Have Fallen Enforcing the Law

LAWRENCE N. BLUM, PH.D.

LANTERN BOOKS

A Division of Booklight, Inc. • New York

2012
Lantern Books
128 Second Place
Brooklyn, NY 11231
www.lanternbooks.com

Printed in the United States of America

Blum, Lawrence N.
Turning tragedy into victory : lessons learned from cops
who have fallen enforcing the law / by Lawrence N. Blum.
p. cm.
Includes bibliographical references.
ISBN 978-1-59056-411-0 (pbk. : alk. paper) — ISBN 978-1-59056-412-7 (ebook)
1. Police—Job stress. 2. Stress (Physiology) 3. Decision making.
I. Title.
HV7936.J63B58 2012
363.201'9—dc23
2012025614

To Dominick Alexander Blum.
And to the memory of those who have fallen protecting the innocent.

TABLE OF CONTENTS

INTRODUCTION

AFTER PARTICIPATING IN TOO MANY MEMORIAL CEREMONIES FOR peace officers, I have come to believe that if surviving officers truly want to honor those who have fallen in the line of duty, then they must learn the important lessons that come from their experiences and commit themselves to the quest for mastery in law enforcement: to turn tragedy into victory.

In 2000, I wrote *Force Under Pressure: How Cops Live and Why They Die* (Lantern Books, 2000) as an effort to change law enforcement's historic avoidance of the psychology of the peace officer. Officers' lack of knowledge and skill in controlling the stress of the moment has increased their risk of being killed or assaulted, or making mistakes that cost them dearly in career or family relationships. In those cases, how much or how little they knew about tactics and procedure did not matter. What mattered was whether they were able to control what their brain and body did in a moment of crisis.

Since the time of writing *Force Under Pressure*, I became more and more concerned that, with all the knowledge possessed by law enforcement trainers, and all the research done that have documented the factors that compromised officers' tactical performance, nothing really has improved in the area of officer safety and survival.

A recent transmission of the Force Science Institute's Newsletter quoted the National Law Enforcement Officers Memorial Fund, noting that, "At the end of June (2011), total duty-related fatalities in the U.S. are up 8% compared to the same time last year, according to preliminary figures from the National Law Enforcement Officers Memorial Fund. Officer murders from gunfire are spiking an alarming 38% increase. If trends hold through

the second half of the year, we could see the worst annual toll in a decade"
(Lewinski, 2007; 2009; 2010).

The first decade of the twenty-first century was replete with articles,
books, and seminars that discussed law enforcement training and safety
issues; and saw several attempts at realistic training that made at least some
reference to the fact that peace officers' exposure to high levels of stress
exerted a degrading or disrupting influence upon their perception, decision
making, and tactical performance. However, written knowledge of the subject and the groundbreaking research performed, for example, by the Force
Science Institute (Lewinski, 2007; 2009; 2010) have been largely ignored in
most police training efforts.

The assumption continues to be made that once an officer has been
taught tactical principles and practices, he or she should be expected to
perform them properly no matter what conditions they encounter. While
verbal and written references are made to attitude and "stress" as important
elements to be considered, the dynamics of officers' reactions to the stress of
the moment has remained a "black hole" that is generally left out of after-
action reports.

Whereas *Force Under Pressure* contained a discussion of the importance
of the mind in police work, *Turning Tragedy into Victory* will identify pitfalls,
errors, and traps that are created when officers lose control over how their
brains and bodies react to unexpected crisis moments. The book contains
information that will explain why and how this lack of control occurs and
provides mental, emotional, and behavioral control tools that have proven
highly effective at enhancing officers' performance; reducing the chance of
officers making a catastrophic mental, emotional, and/or tactical error; and
increasing the viability of their health and well-being.

In the pages that follow, incidents are presented where officers suffered
serious harm in some way. Their stories also describe the struggles they
went through to recover from these wounds. Few who have not been shot,
stabbed, bludgeoned, or damaged in a traffic collision can truly comprehend
the strength, will, and stamina it took for them to make it back to work as a
cop. With one exception (Johannes Mehserle of the Bay Area Rapid Transit Police Department), actual names are not used in this book.

I hope and expect that the reader will not interpret the discussion of these officers' experiences as being critical of those whose stories fill these pages—they are not. But there are important lessons to be learned from what these law enforcers experienced, and communicating those lessons is why I wrote this book.

The primary objective of the book is to integrate law enforcement's knowledge of how to perform effective tactical responses to threat with skills in controlling how officers' brains and bodies react to high levels of stress and crisis exposure. It is within the moment that they are confronted with unanticipated, rapidly changing, or chaotic stress that errors are most likely to be made—actions undertaken that cannot be taken back.

It is not my intent to try to include all of the possible situations in which bad things can happen in law enforcement. The officers who were interviewed for this book were generous enough to share openly their experiences and private pain with people they don't even know. Their message was simple and direct: "Tell other cops how it happened, Doc. I don't want them to have to go through the hell that I've been through."

It is true that some of the bad things that happen in law enforcement are unavoidable. There is always the chance that someone waits in ambush for peace officers and shoots or stabs them without any warning, and without any chance for officers to defend themselves. However, it is also true that most of the damage done to peace officers' lives and careers can be prevented.

In the eleven years since I wrote *Force Under Pressure* a new generation of peace officers has taken the reins in law enforcement. They are equipped with a more advanced technology and powerful information, surveillance, and communication systems to assist them in the performance of their work.

However, the increases in technology have not prevented peace officers from being assaulted and killed at a rate that must one day become unacceptable in a civilized society that prides itself on high moral values. From 2000 to 2009, the Federal Bureau of Investigation reported that 536 American peace officers were murdered in the course of duty. During the same period of time, a greater number, 728 peace officers, were killed in traffic collisions. An average of over 54,000 officers each year were assaulted during this same time period (Federal Bureau of Investigation, Uniform Crime Reports, Law Enforcement Officers Killed and Assaulted, 2009).

THERE IS NO SUCH THING AS FRIENDLY FIRE

A police officer was killed a number of years ago during a SWAT operation in the Southwest. The event underscored the terrible damage that can be done when an officer's level of internal excitation gets so "jacked up" that the actions they take in a tactical encounter are performed without thought, judgment, or self-regulation.

At that time, as is the case with many law enforcement agencies, being a member of a SWAT team was not a full-time assignment. Officers were occupied with other duties until a call came for the team to be mobilized. Members of the team then had to shift their work orientation from patrol and detective functions to special operations that required substantially different actions and procedures than their primary duties.

SWAT teams from a number of police departments were assisting in the arrest of a dangerous fugitive. One of the locations involved in the search was a two-story residence where the suspect was known to have resided.

The SWAT team that was to search that location was made up of skilled veteran police officers that had ultimate confidence in their ability—to the point that, when they observed another team slowly going through a walk-through rehearsal with the plan they had for their assigned function, they pointed at the rehearsing team and laughed, saying, "Look at those guys." Their laughter was soon to be extinguished, however.

The officer who was killed was the newest member of the SWAT team. He was a "hard charger," wanting very much to be given the number-one position on the entry team. He asked the team leader and was granted his request. The team entered the residence and began to clear all areas of the first floor.

After the first floor was searched and cleared, preparations were made to search the second floor. In the plan they decided upon, the officer in the first position had the task of deploying a "flash/bang" grenade and throwing it up the stairs. The blinding light and concussive explosion of the "flash/bang" was intended to disorient the suspect and allow the entry team to get up the stairs and deploy in positions of advantage.

The new SWAT officer was "amped" by the opportunity to take such an active role in his team's operation. His level of excitement was such that, instead of throwing the grenade to the second story and waiting downstairs for the grenade to detonate, he tossed the grenade and immediately rushed up the stairs behind it. It was as if he were trying to race the grenade up the stairs.

Because of the positions they took, and with the intense and rapid movement up the stairs that occurred, the rest of the team had no idea that the officer had rushed upstairs without waiting and without communicating to anyone what he was doing.

One of the other officers on the entry team was now at the top of the stairs on the second-story landing, and was beginning the process of clearing the upstairs bedrooms when he observed a figure walking through the heavy smoke out of one of the rooms, carrying an assault rifle.

There was no way for this officer to know that the figure walking from the room was the young officer whose excitation had triggered his totally unpredictable behavior. In the stress of the moment, that officer, who expected to see a suspect under these conditions, fired at the figure, and the young, overly exuberant SWAT officer was killed. The officers on that SWAT team had a tragic education that day: there is no such thing as friendly fire.

One of the changes made by the grieving police department was assigning officers to the SWAT team on a full-time basis. They learned the importance of walking through and rehearsing each step involved in warrant service, and took their subsequent training with a great deal more seriousness than they had performed when their expectation was that such a tragedy was "not going to happen to us." They still feel the pain of that education several years later.

Because of mandated training content in areas such as ethics, sexual harassment, and cultural diversity—as well as fears that administrators and risk managers have of officers making claims that they were injured in training—most of the officers I have spoken with reported that they trained in a manner that replicated life-threatening conditions about once every one to two years. Only a small number of law enforcement agencies faced the risk of possible I.O.D. (injured on duty) claims from classes that, for example, included sparring or fighting on the ground in order to build proficiency, skill, confidence, and stamina in reacting to lethal levels of threat. In this time of shrinking budgets, the amount of realistic training and preparation for the field or institution has been further reduced.

I was called to help with the aftermath of the murder of a peace officer twenty-six times in the thirty-one years I've spent working with peace officers. I treated or spoke with a great many more officers who were shot, stabbed, or bludgeoned as well. It was difficult to listen to or read the after-incident reports that spoke of what the wounded or murdered officers "could have or should have done differently" that might have prevented the harm that was done. They never spoke about, nor asked, however, *why* the victim officer had made the judgment, or took the action that placed him or her at a greater risk of disadvantage, harm, or defeat.

Was their response to the threat they faced based upon purposeful, controlled mental activity and decision-making? Or were they so driven by a sense of urgency to close in on and seize control of a suspect that they were drawn into a position of danger from which they could not escape?

Did they expect that, because they had had successful contacts in the past with "situations like this," that *this* contact *this* time was going to go the same way? Did they fall into a trap when the conditions turned out to be different and they weren't mentally prepared for it?

Other than the pain that was caused by these harmful, often tragic events, I was struck most by statements made by a majority of the wounded officers with whom I had spoken. They told me that, prior to their contact with the suspect who had harmed them, they had experienced an uncomfortable feeling or sense that "there was something wrong with this picture."

Many of those who serve in law enforcement are in the habit of "gutting through" and paying no attention to internal feelings of concern, uneasiness, or dread about a contact they are about to make. They get into the habit of ignoring feelings of alarm, anxiety, or discomfort, because such reactions are widely viewed in law enforcement as a weakness to be avoided.

They continue at times to use the same tactics they began with, even though some (subconscious) part of their mind and memory senses that those tactics would no longer be viable. Or they remain momentarily frozen in a static, stationary position that increases the danger to them, even though their "gut feeling" is communicating to them that they are in a position of disadvantage and need to move.

The danger to new officers is that they have yet to gain the confidence to listen to their "gut feelings" about something being wrong at a particular scene. The danger to experienced officers is that they may have started to operate on a type of "automatic pilot"; not concentrating upon the current conditions, but instead performing the habitual ways they had worked in the past regardless of the here-and-now conditions (sometimes referred to as complacency or working with "your head up your ass").

Victim officers often acknowledged that they had formed an expectation—that is, a pre-judgment—about the conditions they were about to encounter. Their mind retrieved a memory of similar incidents they encountered in the past and had successfully resolved. Their conscious thoughts were along the lines of, "Oh, it's going to be one of these."

They retrieved these incidents from memory because it made them feel more comfortable and free of the tension and anxiety officers can feel when they approach unknown conditions. Having an expectation of what they would encounter allowed them to feel more in control and confident in their approach. When the actual encounter was different from what they expected, however, they were unable to shift their approach and tactics quickly enough to prevent an assault against them.

Without training and practice to the contrary, the human brain is "wired" to react to unanticipated threat with survival-oriented, instinctive and reflex actions—and not under the conscious control of the individual performing them. During these moments, officers may not be able to apply necessary self-regulation to perform the tactics that they knew or had been trained in, but which were inaccessible to them due to mental, emotional, and behavioral disruption caused by their brain's uncontrolled response to high levels of threat.

FIGHT, FLIGHT, AND FREEZE

After eight years of exemplary police work in a large urban police department in the Southwest, Mark, an experienced and talented police officer, decided to move his family to a suburban community that was far from the high crime activity he was used to. When he first saw his new neighborhood, he joked with his young wife that they had found the real "Mayberry R.F.D." He told her that his biggest task here would be to adjust to the slower pace at his new department. On the day that he was killed, his son was nine months old.

The call received by the police dispatcher came from an employee of an insurance agency. She reported that one of their clients, a resident of the city, was threatening to kill himself. The dispatcher broadcast the call as a possible suicide attempt using pills and alcohol.

It would be logical with this information for responding officers to expect that this subject would be sedated, unconscious, or expired by the time they arrived at the residence. For some unknown reason, the dispatcher did not broadcast the fact that there had been previous police contacts at this address for shots-fired calls.

The plan that was developed had Mark in the rear of the residence just inside the cinder block wall that formed the property boundaries. He was watching the sliding glass door that opened to the rear patio. A sergeant who had been promoted four days earlier was just outside the wall.

Mark was feeling extremely uncomfortable. He had no real cover or concealment in his position, and felt vulnerable where he was. He turned to the new sergeant and said, "My position here stinks." But he *remained still* in that uncomfortable position for a moment too long. He was shot and killed by the individual that had threatened suicide, who then turned the gun on himself.

I visited his young widow and nine-month-old son. The widow told me that they called their son "Bubba," and that he closely resembled the father he would never know.

When an officer experiences a feeling of acute discomfort that "something is wrong with this picture," *their brain is telling them that they are in a position of disadvantage.* Why remain in it? The problem is that there is a strong, instinctive tendency for human beings to temporarily remain in a stationary, static position when they are startled (referred to as "stasis"). This is the behavior that is described by the word "freeze."

But movement away from a compromised position must be conscious and purposeful to overcome the brain's tendency to maintain the individual in stasis due to the shock experienced when it feels unexpectedly threatened, or when a survival-oriented instinct initiates an impulsive, defensive, or withdrawn rather than strategic action.

There is a haunting scene in the movie *Saving Private Ryan* where a cowardly soldier cowers on the staircase, avoiding the room where an American ranger is in hand-to-hand combat with a German soldier. The film shows the aggressive and violent sights and sounds of mortal combat. The American ranger is yelling, growling, and fighting up until the point that the German soldier says something to him.

Then we see the American soldier suddenly stop fighting. In a plaintive-sounding voice, he asks the German soldier, "What did that mean? What did that mean?" He has suddenly and completely stopped all aggression. The extreme effort that characterized his earlier fighting efforts has been extinguished by some apparent need he triggered to "make it stop." The German soldier shushes him, and slowly stabs the American soldier to death with his bayonet.

Officers' expectations—prior to having to fight for their life—that they will not behave in a flight, freeze, or passive way to a lethal threat may not be accurate in those instances where they feel a loss of control over the circumstances they have encountered. The mind will not do what an officer hopes it will do in response to an unexpected lethal threat; it will do what that officer has trained and conditioned it to do over hundreds of repetitions of rehearsal practice.

I teach a class called I've Been Shot! Maintaining the Will to Survive for officers after they have been shot, stabbed, or bludgeoned. A major purpose of the class is to inoculate peace officers against the danger of inadvertently experiencing a *psychology of defeat* when they face what may seem to them to be an overwhelming threat. The term "psychology of defeat" refers to a perception by an individual that "this is too much for me . . . I wasn't ready for this . . . this wasn't supposed to happen. . . ."

As will be discussed later in greater detail, peace officers must, in order to prevent the possibility of a defeatist reaction to an attack against them, engage in continual activities that form victorious habits well before a dangerous contact is faced—that is, performing the purposeful acts of will that prevent their brains from believing that they may not be capable of dealing with the threat in front of them. The purpose here is to prevent any defensive, indecisive, passive, avoidant, or withdrawal behaviors when the threat confronting the officer requires decisive, aggressive, violent action for them to survive.

If officers are not made confident in their ability to manage conditions that replicate those found in the field, or are not given sufficient repetitions of practice, one cannot expect them to attain peak performance in the tasks necessary to achieve safety and proper control of a scene. Some aspect of the officer's tactical response will be compromised, and resistive or assaultive subjects will gain greater initiative control within the encounter (see, e.g., Cannon-Bowers & Salas, 1998).

There is a quote from Vince Lombardi, the coach emeritus of the Green Bay Packers, that exemplifies the importance of the drive to mastery in one's endeavors (his quote leaves out the female gender, which should be included by the reader): "I firmly believe that any man's finest hours—his greatest fulfillment of all that he holds dear—is that moment when he has worked his heart out in good cause and lies exhausted on the field of battle—victorious."

To achieve mastery and excellence in one's life and one's career, however, "just doing okay" or "just passing" cannot be permitted to be acceptable standards for how one works and lives. Peace officers will one day arrive at a fork in the road where they must decide for themselves: "How good is good enough for me? How strong, worthwhile, and victorious do I want my life to be?"

It should become unacceptable in law enforcement organizations to have to wait for more officers to be harmed, ruined, or killed because no one ever trained them how to effectively manage and control their immediate reaction to stressful events.

Tactical principles and officer safety procedures exist to provide peace officers with the advantage over dangerous or disturbed people and situations. They are designed to prevent a successful assault against peace officers. Sometimes, however, an officer's sense of urgency to act—in other words, "the zeal to do the deal"—violates those principles. When in hot pursuit of a suspect, or during undercover narcotics activities, for example, violations of officer safety occur that drastically increase the risk of harm.

Although police officers are provided with tools and taught procedures with the expectation that they will be proficient and controlled in their use, it is rare for a law enforcement agency to provide its officers with proficiency in the use of mental controls to ensure that the individual responds to threat with accurate perceptions, effective judgment, critical decision-making, and strategic actions appropriate to circumstance.

I believe that it is critical for peace officers to learn and practice the tools that will ensure a strategic, rather than impulsive or delayed reaction to threat. In addition, mental processes must be learned and conditioned by officers so that they can be provided with the ability to mitigate the harm to their health caused by traumatic events.

By habituating themselves to the use of conscious mental controls during times of duress, officers will add to and alter the nerve connections in their brains and form habits that prevent them from losing control when the "Oh, shit!" moments of law enforcement occur.

The fact that peace officers' contact with continuing stress exposure and trauma causes physical and emotional injury has been documented in several studies (see, e.g., Violanti et al., 1986; van der Kolk et al., 1988, 1991; Blum, 1998). That is, there is a physical and emotional price that peace officers pay because of inescapable and damaging conditions they encounter in the course of their work. Rarely, however, are peace officers prepared psychologically for traumatic events and stress exposure, and so do not minimize and extinguish the harmful impact of these work conditions.

1

"THERE IS SOMETHING WRONG WITH THIS PICTURE"

IT WAS MOTHER'S DAY, MAY 14, 2007. PETE WAS UNDECIDED ABOUT going to work that night. He decided to go in for the second half of his shift. The night had been quiet. Pete and his partner were relatively new to each other. They had worked together for four months in the detective division, but had been on the same tactical team some months before.

The two detectives were at the bottom of the duty list that assigned cases on this date. They were assigned to the robbery unit of a large urban police department in the Midwest, but continued to work the streets looking for dope and guns whenever they could. They both felt pride at having gotten many guns and drugs off the streets during their years on patrol and the gang detail, and they continued their active police work on the robbery team.

The two of them had seized one hundred pounds of marijuana one week earlier. A supervisor had taken a picture of the seizure and called the commander of their division at home. The commander was pleased with the arrest and happily took credit for the seizure, thus sparing Pete and his partner repercussions from their "being somewhat off the reservation" (they were not assigned to narcotics enforcement at the time).

They had decided to end their night with a drive through a high-crime area, to look for a good arrest on the way back to the station. The street they drove toward was notorious for drug dealing and for the high number of unsolved murders perpetrated there. A gang that controlled this part of the city was suspected of committing many of the area's crime.

A number of gang members had been charged with murder but were either acquitted or had the charges dismissed due to witness reluctance or disappearance. The individual who later shot Pete in the back was wanted on two separate felony warrants, a circumstance that should, theoretically, have been impossible. He had recently been discharged from parole, through a number of justice system failures or errors.

Pete had worked this street quite often during the years he was assigned to the gang unit and plainclothes street crime suppression team. He and his partner turned the corner, passing a house well-known to the police for gang activity. They saw three males standing on the porch and one male standing on the sidewalk in front of it. As soon as the males observed the darkened police vehicle, the one who had stood on the porch went inside, leaving two males standing there. The individual on the sidewalk quickly began to walk down the street away from the house.

His actions were characteristic of someone carrying a gun or dope. Pete smiled at his partner and said, "Let's follow this one and see what he's got that he doesn't want us to find." Pete was driving very slowly, watching as the male walked down the sidewalk. The young male was looking straight ahead, as if he was unaware of the police vehicle that paralleled his path. He stopped at a gate halfway down the block and pretended to be fumbling with a key to open the lock.

"Look at that asshole," Pete said to his partner, laughing. "As soon as I crack this door, he's going to bolt."

Pete stopped the police car and opened the door to get out. As soon as he did, the young male took off, running back up the street toward the house in front of which the other gang members had been standing.

Pete was a hard-nosed, proactive police officer. He led the units he worked for in arrests and seizures of guns. He was in his thirties and still could run down those who ran from him. He had never quit in a chase or a fight, and had never really experienced defeat in police work or in life. While he resisted admitting it to me, he acknowledged that, prior to being shot, he thought that he could not be beaten or stopped, as if a big red *S* was painted on the shirt he wore beneath his ballistic vest.

His focus of attention was locked on catching the young male, so he took off running after him without hesitation or discussion with his partner. He did not know where his partner was. He assumed that his partner was running behind him, as Pete was a faster runner. There was a vacant lot next to the corner that led to an alley behind the houses on the street. The youth ran into and through the lot in an attempt to reach the alley and escape.

In fact, Pete's partner had run back to their police car to try to flank the gang member with their car to stop him. One of the problems with his plan, however, was the fact that Pete automatically took the car keys with him when he began to chase someone. He had learned to remove the keys from the ignition when he stopped his car in neighborhoods such as this one, so that the vehicle would still be there upon his return. His partner did not know this and, in the heat of the moment, they had not communicated with each other about their plans of action. Without either of them intending it, Pete was now left on his own.

As Pete ran past the house, he saw in his peripheral vision that the two males who had been standing on the porch were watching him pass by. "That's funny," Pete remembers thinking at the time, "they usually run when they see us coming."

The two gang members he had observed in passing walked down the steps of the house and turned in the direction that Pete was heading. One of them aimed a .45 caliber semi-automatic pistol at the officer they saw chasing their "homie." One shot was fired. Pete heard a booming sound that he remembers as being extremely loud. His initial thought was that someone had fired at his partner. He started to turn his head to see what was happening behind him, but found himself falling hard to the ground. He had been shot in the back— just above his belt line and just below the ballistic vest he was wearing. The bullet fragmented when it entered Pete's body, with one part severing part of his colon, and the other entering his bladder.

His body quickly began to swell with trauma and internal bleeding. He began to feel incredible pain. He felt his pants and shirt filling with his blood. He thought he was going to die.

As he felt the flood of pain and saw the amount of blood coming out of him, he was struck by a powerful sense of irony. "Now I get shot? This isn't supposed to happen now. I've got ten years on and am a robbery detective and I finished working the streets in patrol and crime suppression work. I'm going to die now in a garbage-filled lot on Mother's Day."

Like many detectives, Pete believed that if he were going to get shot, it would only happen when he was a young, aggressive patrol officer free from major family responsibilities. After trying for a number of years, he and his wife now had a fifteen-month-old son. This was the last day of Pete's work-week, and he had planned to take his son to the zoo the next day.

I want to see my son again, he thought. *I have to see my son again.* He was getting light-headed from the loss of blood. He called in the message that chills the souls of those who serve in law enforcement: "Officer down . . . Shots fired . . . I've been shot! I'm in a lot off the corner of _____ Street . . . I need an ambulance. . . ." He tried to put his radio back in its pocket but found that his ability to control what he did with his hands was impaired.

He was able to take out the card of St. Michael, patron saint of police officers, that he always kept in his front pocket, and held it tightly in his hand. His partner now rushed up to him, breathing heavily. Pete remembers how "amped" his partner was. He was committed to catching the person who had shot his partner.

"F__k him," answered Pete. "I need help!" But his partner took off and ran in the direction in which the fleeing male had gone. Pete thought he was bleeding out and was scared. After what seemed like several minutes' time, he heard the sound of police sirens. While he was greatly pleased to hear "the cavalry" coming, he had also lost patience lying there. *I don't need cops now, I already got shot. Now I need a freakin' ambulance.* Pete was committed that he was not going to die there and lose his family. He became unsettled, however, when the first officer arrived.

The officer who reached him first was someone that he knew. This person had just returned to work after over a year's absence from work because he had developed a brain tumor. Pete had not heard what had happened to him, and had thought perhaps he had died. The officer took the card with St. Michael's prayer from Pete's hand, and began to read:

Saint Michael the Archangel, defend us in battle. Be our protection against the wickedness and snares of the devil. May God rebuke him, we humbly pray; and do Thou, O Prince of the Heavenly Host, by the Divine Power of God, cast into hell Satan and all the evil spirits who roam throughout the world seeking the ruin of souls.

That's it, Pete thought. *I'm dead. That's why this guy is here. He's already dead and now I am.* He was going into shock from loss of blood and lowered blood pressure. The fact that he was feeling agonizing pain eventually reassured him. He couldn't be dead if he was in this much pain.

Other officers were now at his side. "Don't go to sleep," they yelled to him. "Stay with us . . . you're going to be okay . . . just don't go to sleep!"

His older brother was also a police officer in the department and was working patrol at the time that he was shot. His brother responded to the call of an officer down that had been put out on multiple frequencies by a dispatcher. He was not aware that it was his brother who had been shot. It was after he arrived at the scene and began searching for the shooter that another officer grabbed him and brought him to Pete's side.

Pete's brother got in the ambulance that was transporting Pete to the trauma center at the county hospital. During the drive to the hospital, Pete heard his brother's voice on the telephone: "Mom, put Dad on the phone. Dad, Peter's been shot . . . in the back . . . he's going to County. . . ."

Both brothers knew how much their mother worried about the safety of the men in her life. Pete's father, a decorated Vietnam combat veteran, had spent twenty-nine years of service as a special agent for the F.B.I. His brother had served as a U.S. Marine and then followed his younger brother into the city's police department.

Pete arrived at the county hospital's trauma center. There were other patients on gurneys in the area. He heard a doctor talking to another person close by: "His wife is here, I think we should let her come to see him."

"We don't have time," said the other doctor, "we have to get him into surgery."

Pete remembers thinking, *Why don't they let the poor bastard see his wife?*

In the next moment his wife was at his side. He found it ironic. *Now I'm the poor bastard I have so often seen on gurneys in trauma rooms like this.*

"I'm so sorry," he said to his wife.

She touched his forehead and told him, "Don't be sorry. I'm proud of you."

The sweetness of her statement brought him a great deal of comfort and relief. That comment was just the beginning of his wife's support throughout the agony of his recovery. Her being there when it counted stays with Pete always.

Everything went dark again after the trauma center staff took him into surgery. He came to in the recovery room. He spent moments not knowing where he was or why he was there. Then, he remembered that he had been shot. He knew that he was alive, but felt detached from his body lying in the bed.

A few moments later, a doctor appeared at his bedside and introduced himself as the lead surgeon in the team that had performed his operation. The doctor started to speak with him but stopped a number of times, hesitant, as if he were reporting something he was not comfortable with.

Pete became very frightened. He thought that the doctor was about to tell him that he was paralyzed. The doctor then got out that they had to perform a colostomy and Pete was going to have to wear and use a colostomy bag on a temporary basis. His feeling of relief that he would walk again began a series of major ups and downs through the long and difficult process of his recovery.

Some of his wounds were visible. They had entry marks and scars to prove their existence. Other wounds, however, did not have any entry marks. They had to do with the loss of feelings of self-confidence that had always come naturally to Pete before he was shot, and a difficulty with being decisive that he had never felt before.

In the days following the surgery, Pete's awareness of how close he had come to dying hit home. He questioned himself about the worth of the things he had accomplished as a police officer. He began to believe that police work was not worth dying for—orphaning his children, making a widow of his wife for neighborhoods and people who did not have anything to do with his life or the life of his loved ones.

After two weeks in intensive care, he transferred to the university hospital because of his need for a number of specialists. Pieces of the bullet still remained in his bladder and hip.

Though it is not something that he thought about in the early days of his recovery, Pete was about to discover the reality of risk management efforts on the part of his city. At his first meeting with the doctors who would be attending his treatment and recovery, a woman appeared and sat down with Pete, his wife, and their doctors. She introduced herself as the case management person employed by the city. She told him that her job was to monitor every treatment or rehabilitation session he attended, to "minimize the costs of your treatment and to see you get back to work as quickly as possible." Thus began what became the most bitter part of his recovery.

There are differences in how risk management is performed by the municipalities, counties, and states that have become self-insured due to the ever-increasing premiums for workers' compensation and liability insurance. In some jurisdictions case managers, who are often trained medical professionals, take a supportive approach to injured officers' rehabilitation. In other jurisdictions, claims for workers' compensation are contested as a matter of policy and strategy. When an injured peace officer's employer takes the latter approach, the efforts that are intended to work toward officers returning to duty as quickly as possible can result in an exacerbation of the difficulties involved in their recovery. In these cases, an adversarial, counterproductive relationship is developed between the injured officer and his or her employer.

The case manager in Pete's case established a pattern of questioning— that is, contesting—his doctors' treatment plans and findings. She kept repeating the same question in each meeting he had with one of his doctors or physical therapists: "When can he return to work?" In a number of Pete's treatment sessions with his doctors, her intrusive questioning required the doctors to ask her to leave so they could do their work with their patient.

Pete recalls being angry and frustrated with the city's methods of responding to his injuries. He lived in constant pain, and continued to experience a great deal of emotional distress. He felt guilty for putting his family through the hell of nearly losing him.

His recovery was characterized by phases in which he experienced a range of conflicted thoughts and emotions: "I was elated at first . . . I wasn't para-lyzed, but I didn't want to get up and do anything." He developed doubts about whether being a cop was worth the pain and fear of being shot again.

He remembers talking with the police chaplain. The priest had asked him when he thought he would be ready to return to police work. His response surprised him: "Father, I'm not sure I'm going to go back to work as a police officer. I was unreasonable . . . selfish, doing the things I was doing. This was my wake-up call. I would have kept doing it until I got killed."

Covered in bandages, he was transported home. He had been away for several weeks. The day he left the hospital, he refused to use a wheelchair. He walked haltingly and with some support, but it was very important to him to walk out of the hospital doors that he had been wheeled into on a gurney.

His son became frightened and began to cry when they brought him to Pete. Pete was determined that his son would again know and love him, and that he would not put his family in jeopardy again. He felt fairly certain in the early parts of his recovery that he would not return to work as a police officer. "I didn't think I would go back until three months before I did go back. My thought then was that I would retire, receive seventy-five percent of my salary, and be a dad. But I couldn't see myself doing any of the things I had thought about doing as an alternative to police work."

The city ordered an evaluation of his injuries by their contracted doctor. This occurred at Christmastime, seven months after he was shot. Pete was greatly disturbed by this order: "I felt mistreated . . . like they thought I was malingering. I wasn't ready to go back and didn't want to put my life in the hands of some city doctor." He did, however, show up for the appointments.

After being sent for several opinions, he was asked by one doctor how much longer he thought he needed to prepare physically to return to work. He told the doctor that he had not been able to run yet and would like to try and run for at least a month, and then if all went well he would go back. Two weeks later, the department medical section called Pete's house and left a message saying, "Congratulations! You have been cleared for full duty. Report on Monday."

"My wife cried," Pete told me. "It was the week before Christmas.

I thought about my options and realized that while I did in fact feel pretty good physically, I had zero interest in going back to work. I would rather take my son to museums, play with his building blocks in the basement and read him book after book at night. I was not ready to say good night to him at night and then walk out the door to go drive around some neighborhood where no one I cared about lived."

Before he got shot, Pete had taken for granted that he would always feel confident in his work. But he was no longer feeling certain of what to do, or confident of his ability to perform. He wondered if it was worth it to be at risk of putting his loved ones through grief just to perform the work that he had once loved.

He knew he was not psychologically prepared to go back to work. He did not report. Shortly thereafter, an inspector from the police department telephoned his home and told his wife that Pete was in violation of a direct order. Pete's wife was in a panic. Were they now in trouble with the department in addition to the stress of his physical and mental recovery?

Pete immediately telephoned the inspector and told him that he had made an appointment with the director of the department's Employee Assistance Program (EAP) and would not return to work until he'd been cleared by her. The inspector replied in a derisive manner, "Oh, you're going that route." Pete was ordered to call the inspector after every doctor or physical therapy visit he made.

When he first contacted the director of the EAP, he asked her if it was mandatory that he seek professional help before he returned to work. She told him that it was not necessary, although it would be a good idea to do so. She told him that there was no requirement to see a professional if you were shot; only if you shot someone else. He then asked her, "Who's to say I won't go back and shoot everybody I see? I'm not saying I would, but how does anybody know that I won't?"

She then invited him to come in to talk with her, and she became very helpful to him in his recovery. She "ran interference" for him with the department while he did the work necessary to get his "edge back," and ultimately allowed him to decide when he felt capable of returning to work: "She told me to come in a few weeks after Christmas and to tell the inspector who was now leaving messages at my house that I was under her care and when I was cleared for duty by her, she would notify the chain of command."

Pete returned to police duties in March 2008, ten months after he'd been shot. He was tentative at first: "I didn't want to arrest people or do police work. Now I want to work . . . I do it smarter now. I see the bigger picture."

Pete described the ambivalent feelings that many wounded officers experience in their efforts to return to work: "I get scared shitless . . . I'm still terrified at the last moment. [But] I make the willful decision to do it. Two to three weeks after I went back to the streets, I knew that this is what I'm supposed to be doing. I'm good at it. I got back the confidence I lost when I was shot. I can do things that matter in places that matter."

Pete joined a Violent Criminal Apprehension Task Force coordinated by the F.B.I. and went after murderers and perpetrators of child sexual assault. He told me a truth that was ugly to him: "I feel at the top of my game, but at the moment before going in the door, I think, 'this is it.' Is this (arrest) worth it if it goes bad? With all the tech stuff, 'pinging' phones to locate crooks, it still winds up with you climbing a ladder into an attic or going down into a basement after a bad guy."

One of the aftereffects of his injuries is that Pete is a much wiser police officer. He now pays very close attention to feelings of uneasiness that "something is wrong with this picture." His pain and his success in overcoming the obstacles to return to work have made him much more focused and vigilant in how he performs police duties.

Before a person seriously "gets their butt kicked," they are much more likely to be influenced by the thrill of the chase, and not by a slowing or lessening of drive within themselves that is achieved by considering the consequences of their actions. There is also a great deal of social support in law enforcement for "toughing it out" through dangerous conditions. The clear expectation exists that officers must not let something like a distressed emotion weaken their resolve. They are tasked with confronting danger and must not be distracted by the fear, anxiety, or dread that immobilizes most human beings when they are exposed to threat.

After the painful lessons learned when officers are seriously wounded or injured, they are much more willing to be conscious and vigilant when an internal discomfort tells them that they are in a position of disadvantage. How sad it is that this wisdom in law enforcement often doesn't come until severe damage is done.

Controlling the surge of internal excitation sufficiently to maintain vigilance, self-regulation, and tactical control is the "holy grail" to be sought by peace officers. There are dangerous pitfalls that await the officers who, because they are "jacked up" or driven by the "thrill of the chase" do not alter their position, plan, or tactics once danger signals appear. Ignoring internal signals of danger is an act that is easy to fall into and a herculean effort from which to recover.

As noted elsewhere, the exposure to stress results in a narrowing or blocking of the senses. This reflex reaction to stress includes a lessening in concentration upon internal emotional and/or physical activity. Therefore, peace officers must be practiced and proficient at monitoring their internal reactivity as well as external conditions to maximize their safety and the chances for victory and success. Trust your gut reactions! They are your best ally when you are in a position where a sensed but unseen danger lurks.

2

STRESS EXPOSURE

IMPACT UPON SENSES, THINKING, AND ACTIONS

Peace officers usually have little or no difficulty managing events where the conditions they encounter are expected, or when they have sufficient time to assess the event and make decisions. Even though their ability to manage crises with no degradation in performance is critical to the outcome of events, the level of officers' proficiency in managing their exposure to severe stress has been, in many cases, insufficient.

It is assumed that once officers acquire and retain knowledge of tactical principles and practices, they should be able to use that knowledge effectively—without the necessity for developing an accompanying proficiency in managing stress exposure—in whatever circumstances they encounter in the course of their duty. Acting under this assumption has been damaging to too many of those who serve in law enforcement.

Peace officers' exposure to stressful conditions very often causes change and distortion in how their brain perceives the things that their eyes see, that their ears hear, et cetera. Exposure to stress alters how their brain processes the information that they received from their assessment of the environment. Even in those instances where officers actually did respond properly to a threat encounter within the guidelines of law, policy, and training, the unanticipated effects of that stress exposure upon officers' perception, judgment, decision-making, memory, and performance can change their lives forever.

"I'm going to tase him! I'm going to tase him!"

One of the more recent tragic events in law enforcement occurred in the Bay Area of central California on New Year's morning, 2009. Johannes Mehserle was a police officer working for the Bay Area Rapid Transit Police Department (BART PD) in California until January 1, 2009, when the life he had been living abruptly came to a halt. One uncontrolled act under conditions of severe stress resulted in catastrophic consequences for him, his family, and the BART Police Department—a department that was deeply torn by this incident and its aftermath.

A fight had broken out on a BART commuter train late on New Year's Eve, 2008. The train's engineer called for police assistance. The BART police officers that responded removed a number of people who had participated in the disturbance from the train. These individuals cooperated with officers, and no uses of force occurred. However, a young male, Oscar Grant III, age twenty-two, refused to comply with the commands that were given to him.

For several weeks prior to January 1, 2009, BART officers had been finding guns at an alarming rate on people who were riding the trains. Officers often talked with one another about how dangerous their patrol beat had become. Indeed, a BART police officer's backup can be fifteen to twenty minutes away by train.

In the midst of a crowd of people who were videotaping and yelling at them, Officer Mehserle and his partner were attempting to place handcuffs on Mr. Grant, whom they had placed on the ground on his stomach. Grant kept his right hand underneath his body and was moving it. The screaming of the crowd and the struggle for control with this noncompliant individual sent Officer Mehserle's stress levels extremely high. At one point in the struggle, he decided that a greater force option was needed to bring Mr. Grant into compliance.

He was experiencing serious alarm. While he made no verbal communication about it to his partner, he believed that Mr. Grant's actions meant that he had a gun in his possession. In his perception, this was no longer just an attempt to bring a resistive subject into compliance. He perceived that he was in life-threatening danger and called out to his partner, "I'm going to tase him! I'm going to tase him."

Peace officers' education and training do not familiarize them or teach them how to understand and control the extreme emotions they may experience during moments of crisis. Many do not realize that unexpected emotions can create a perception of reality that is not objectively present, but which they respond to as if the perceived conditions are actually happening.

In these moments, the parts of the brain that form conscious intent are overcome by "fight or flight," the survival-oriented stress response that is instinctively ignited when the individual perceives severe and imminent threat. Officer Mehserle had no conscious awareness that, instead of his intended act to deploy the electric barbs from his taser, he drew his firearm. He shot the unarmed Mr. Grant once. The bullet entered his back and killed him.

Two experts in peace officers' use of force, Dr. Bill Lewinski (director of the Force Science Institute) and Capt. (retired) Greg Myers (past Commander of Los Angeles Police Department's Police Academy) testified in Officer Mehserle's criminal trial. They noted that Officer Mehserle "had scant experience with drawing or using a taser, none of it in stressful circumstances. He'd carried a taser while working only about ten times. He had drawn it in training half a dozen times, and on duty perhaps three times. By contrast, he'd been drawing his firearm an estimated fifty times a week in practice since graduating from the academy about two years earlier. He'd practiced drawing very fast and had built a strong automatic motor program" (Lewinski, 2010).

According to my personal communications with BART Police Association board members and command personnel, the incident tore the department apart. In the throes of his anguish, Officer Mehserle followed an attorney's advice a few days afterwards and engaged in another impulse-driven action. He resigned from his employment as a BART police officer. In doing so, he gave up the protections (albeit slim) that are afforded peace officers in the performance of their duties.

Officer Mehserle was indicted, tried in criminal court and, amid rioting and demonstrations demanding that he pay dearly for a totally unintended discharge of his firearm, was found guilty of involuntary manslaughter and sentenced to two years in prison.

In an article he wrote about the testimony he gave in Johannes Mehserle's criminal trial, Captain Myers noted that "I also testified about BART's training, which did not put trainees through stress-inducing scenarios." Myers went on to state that "It is essential that trainers put officers through their paces with training that is dynamic, stress-inducing, and requires officers to make quick force-options decisions. The training must truly test the officer's ability to be ready for stressful encounters on the street" (Myers, (2010).

I agree with Captain Myers that peace officers' training must be performed in a manner that replicates—as much as is possible—the conditions they will encounter in the field or institution. But I also believe that training that will "truly test the officer's ability to be ready for stressful encounters on the street" is not easily performed when the emphasis of the training is solely upon the tactics that are performed.

Peace officers must also be made conversant with how their brain and bodies react to an unexpected exposure to stress. They must be given control tools and methods that enable them to mediate the heightened stress in order to maintain effective and purposeful self-regulation.

The negative consequences of an inability to manage the stress of the moment can also be observed in sensory distortions and shock reactions that officers very often experience in the midst of their response to an unexpected threat. In reality, whether or not peace officers perform the correct actions in a crisis, it is the content of their verbal and written reports that will determine whether their actions are to be judged as justified. Any sensory distortions, gaps in their recollection, or mental uncertainty and confusion they experience can result in horrific consequences to them and their families.

NO GOOD DEED GOES UNPUNISHED

Don became a district attorney's investigator after serving twenty-eight years as a sheriff's investigator working primarily with child abuse and child sexual assault cases. He was a gentle and kindhearted person, not the usual stereotype of a warrior in law enforcement. He was active in his church, and it would be hard to find someone there who didn't think the world of him.

In 2003, Don was given the assignment of picking up the two children of a female who had absconded with them from a Child Protective Service (CPS) foster placement. She had a history of law violations and was a known methamphetamine addict. Since it was assumed that the warrant service was a low-risk enforcement activity, a civilian employee accompanied Don. He did not expect the children to be with the woman, but he was given information that she was coming to the County Rescue Mission to pick up a welfare check.

He parked his vehicle near the Rescue Mission to wait for her. He never saw her entering the Mission, but was called by a welfare worker that worked there and notified him that she was inside. He drove to the parking lot of the Mission and went inside to contact her. He left his mobile phone charging in the car, as it had very little battery power left.

He found the woman and told her that he had to take the children back to Child Protective Services. She started crying and asked if there was anything she could do to keep her children. She told him she had taken a bus to get to the Mission. He responded that he would go with her to CPS to see if she could work something out with the child-care workers. He was aware that she had been accompanied by a parolee boyfriend and was concerned about him due to his history of violence and assault.

As Don was accompanying the woman out of the building, they were accosted by her boyfriend, who yelled, "What the f__k is going on!"

The woman yelled to him, "They're taking me to jail!"

"The f__k they are!" he shouted.

He grabbed the woman and began to push her toward the pickup truck in which they had arrived, which was parked at the side of the Mission entrance. There was a second man, who was seated behind the steering wheel of the truck.

Don quickly approached them and grabbed the boyfriend by the arm. As he did so, he saw the two children in the front seat of the pickup. The boyfriend threw a roundhouse punch at him. Don was able to block the punch with his arm, but the force of the blow knocked him hard against the side of the truck and he fell to the ground. The boyfriend pushed the woman into the cab of the pickup truck and got in the passenger-side door. The children were now between the woman and the driver of the pickup truck.

Don tossed his car keys to the employee who had accompanied him, and told him to "Get me backup now!" He assumed that the civilian employee would comply with his request and that backup would be coming soon. He walked to the driver's side window and identified himself as a peace officer.

The parolee boyfriend began to yell to the driver to "Go! Just go!" Don saw that the driver was under the influence. He walked to the front of the vehicle and pulled out his gun from its holster. He spoke to the driver, attempting to calm things down, telling him that he was not in trouble at this point and not to do anything that would cause him to be arrested.

The parolee boyfriend began yelling at this point: "Run him over! Kill him! Kill him! Run him over!" Don was acutely aware that the two children were seated in the front cab of the pickup truck. He was not about to do anything to place them in jeopardy. He had devoted his entire adult life to protecting children.

The driver started the truck's engine. Don fired two shots, one into the right and one into the left front tires, in an attempt to prevent the truck from leaving. The truck went in reverse and crashed into the line of cars parked behind it. Don again approached the pickup truck and attempted to calm things down. When the driver didn't obey him, he again fired two bullets, one each into the right and left front tires.

The parolee boyfriend was still screaming at the driver to run over Don and kill him. He heard the sound of the engine revving up louder and higher. The truck accelerated toward him. He believed that he was about to be killed.

As the truck reached him, he jumped and turned around in his attempt to avoid being struck. Everything went in slow motion. He felt disoriented. He was totally unaware that, as he turned, he had fired a fifth bullet from his gun. The bullet entered the driver's side window and killed the driver. Don believed that he had only fired four times.

Don went down onto his knees. He watched the truck pass him and crash into a parked car. The passenger-side door opened. He rushed to the vehicle to get the children out of danger. The parolee boyfriend shoved Don, who then brought his gun down on the parolee's head. The parolee pushed him to the ground. The gun fell with Don, and everything slowed down again in Don's mind. He dove to get the gun and saw the parolee run away.

Several police vehicles arrived then, and a helicopter hovered over the parking lot. The helicopter's downdraft blew the expended shell casings from the places Don remembered being when he fired at the truck's tires.

He was shocked when sheriff's investigators told him they had found additional shell casings to the four shots that he had reported firing. He was confused about the events that had occurred. He was in a state of shock that distorted and impaired his awareness and memory of the incident. He could not remember what had happened when he was trying to avoid being hit by the truck.

Two days later, Don was telephoned at work by his longtime colleague, the chief of investigators for another county's district attorney's bureau of investigation. She told him that from what she had heard, everything looked copacetic, but she wanted to know from him what had happened. His response was confused: "I just don't know. I wasn't trying to shoot anybody. But the guy is dead so I must have shot him. I was the only one with a gun so it must have been me. That's why I am looking forward to the walk-through so I can find out what happened." The investigator's longtime colleague contacted the State Attorney General's office and reported that she had concerns about the investigator's comments, that there appeared to be serious problems with this shooting incident. She requested that an investigation begin into Don's actions during the incident.

In the aftermath of the shooting, Don remained in a state of shock. He had just psychologically experienced his own imminent death, and was confused in his speech. Above all, he did not remember shooting the fifth bullet. State investigators later concluded that the first four shots he fired were justified. The fifth bullet he shot—the one that resulted in the death of the driver—was determined to have been in violation of the law.

Based upon the results of the state's investigation, the grand jury indicted Don. The judge hearing the case in the criminal trial would not allow testi-

mony or evidence about distortions in officer perception and memory during lethal force encounters. The judge's statement to the jury and courtroom
was, "No cop is going to be given any special consideration in this court
when they kill somebody. He will be tried just like anyone else." The judge
then turned to Don and said, "You're no different than Joe the ragpicker."
The jury found him guilty of involuntary manslaughter.

Don was sentenced to seven years in the state of California's prison system. He served the maximum amount of his sentence for attempting to save
and protect children who were being endangered by the actions of a violent
felon and drug addict. Since a gun was used in the actions he performed,
he was found liable for an enhancement to the sentence. He was required
to serve 80 percent of his sentence, much longer than most criminals are
incarcerated. I will not forget the visit I made to this fine and honorable
man in prison for as long as I live. This case was the biggest miscarriage of
justice I have ever seen.

Don was released on August 21, 2010, back to a world that now appears
strange and foreign to him. He was victimized by the very system to which
he had devoted so much of his life.

An analogy can be made between the conscious, "thinking brain" of
human beings and a twelve-cylinder engine. This is the part of the brain that
engages in purposeful, intentional mental activity that forms the executive
functions of conscious thought, intent, prioritizing and organizing actions,
and intentional control of behaviors. The thinking brain registers awareness
of events in the environment, assesses those events for threat severity and
imminence, retrieves past learning from memory, chooses among a range
of alternative force options for responding to threats, and organizes and
directs behaviors to take a decided-upon course of action.

Now think of removing eight cylinders' worth of spark and fuel from the
thinking brain, and transferring that brain activity to the parts of the brain
that initiate fear, worry, anger, and emergency arousal—that is, the survival-
oriented, instinctive "fight or flight" activities. With two-thirds of its spark
and fuel removed from the thinking brain, distortions, delay, and disturbance can occur that compromise the accuracy with which the individual
perceives, remembers, judges, and performs.

EMOTIONS AND THREAT

The exposure to stress can trigger intense emotional reactions as an integral component of the survival response (e.g., fear or anger). Emotions exist to provide clues that allow us to appraise possible threats or pressures in the environment. They play an important role in forming expectations used to predict events and enhance people's ability to adapt and respond to encountered conditions (Oatley, Keltner, & Jenkins, 2006).

But emotions, in addition to helping people respond to external pressures or threats, have a powerful and often distorting effect upon how individuals see, think, judge, and respond to those conditions. Several studies have shown that high levels of stress lead to a disorganized and degraded ability to focus attention, process the information available at a scene, judge its severity and imminence, and make decisions (Janis & Mann, 1977; Janis, Defares, & Grossman, 1983; Keinan 1987, 1988).

Studies of emotion-guided threat detection document that emotional states, expectations, and stereotypes held about individuals' ethnicity or appearance caused substantial errors in subjects discriminating guns from such neutral objects as wallets, radios, or keys held in a subject's hand (Baumann & DeSteno, 2010).

Individuals who experience a surge of internal excitation, under-regulated anger, or anxiety at being threatened have a tendency toward narrowing their field of vision—that is, examining fewer alternatives for what actions they can take—and their examination of available options is less systematic and effective than non-threatened individuals.

The fact that peace officers are conditioned to ignore distressed emotions does not mean that they go away. Rather, they exert a now *unconscious influence* upon the officer. And it is not only in the area of personal and family health where the officer is injured by his or her exposure to uncontrolled severe stress. The "emotional baggage" carried by peace officers strongly affects what they perceive and how they react during tactical encounters.

Maybe they were involved in a physical altercation in which their control over a suspect was seriously threatened. The anxiety and anger that they felt at that moment—because cops expend such a substantial effort to tamp down such emotions—are now more likely to occur again in subsequent events without officers being aware of the actual source of those emotions, and require less severity to trigger them.

These are the dynamics that are often present when an officer who managed his or her work in a calm, poised, and controlled manner now appears to be over-reacting to conditions that to others did not appear to require that level of response. As such officers feel distressed or angry emotions, they focus their attention upon a currently encountered condition or person. Then, by a process called projection, they perceive the source of their heightened sense of impatience, anger, or irritability in the current condition rather than more accurately recognizing that they are actually re-experiencing a memory of the past.

They may, for example, have just come home from some harrowing, unsettling, or dangerous experience and carried the memory of those events with them. Officers rarely if ever verbalize the events they encountered at work or the emotions those events created in them. All that one of their family members has to do is make a comment that irritates the officer, and "stand by."

The intense "baggage of the day" carried home with them can easily be attached to the comment a family member makes, resulting in an excessive discharge of often damaging emotion: "Do you see now? This is why I get pissed off around here. You guys cause all my anger!"

THE "FREEZE" COMPONENT OF FIGHT OR FLIGHT

Still other officers may, in response to the sudden introduction of an unexpected threat, remain immobile for a split second as a component of transient shock. When officers are startled, for example, a momentary stasis—being frozen in place—most often accompanies their "Oh, shit!" reaction, delaying their ability to respond.

Unanticipated and rapidly changing threat conditions require an immediate and intentional shift or change in officers' approach to a scene or individual, and the tactics they perform. The danger to officers will be heightened if they remain with their original approach when the new threat requires a substantially different strategy.

There are a number of critical mental tasks for an officer to perform in a confrontation with unanticipated or rapidly changing conditions. First, they must consciously register the new threat in their mind. They must assess the threat for its severity and imminence, decide upon a new tactical response to the new conditions, and then organize their mind and body to enact the new tactical response.

How rapidly and accurately the officer is able to perform the above mental tasks will determine, to a large extent, that officer's victory or defeat. If the officer is unprepared for the change or is hesitant in altering his or her approach (e.g., due to long-held habits in how they perform their work), rapidly changing conditions can make it more difficult for him or her to prioritize the direction, type, intensity, and pace of his or her actions. In this situation, the officer is not acting upon the threat, because he or she is first reacting to it.

The management of a police encounter in the field does not occur with the same stable pattern or predictability and controlled rate of tempo found in the classroom. Proficiency in managing rapidly changing, chaotic, or unanticipated threat incidents requires that officers develop a skill called *adaptive expertise*. This term refers to the ability of an individual to respond to unexpected difficulties by way of a shift in their thinking, demeanor, approach, and tactics *in real time* to solve the problems associated with an unanticipated threat—with no loss of mental accuracy, tactical propriety, or pace.

Routine expertise is based upon the application of previously learned skills. As long as those skills are applicable to the problem faced, past experience is all that is required. Among the advantages observed in routine expertise, experts notice features and meaningful patterns of information that are not noticed by novices; experts can retrieve from memory relevant knowledge quickly and with little attentional effort; and experts tend toward routinization and automaticity in their performance, which increases speed and efficiency (Bransford et al., 2000; see also Chi, Glaser, & Farr, 1988).

Should the conditions an officer encounters require a different approach than what they've been used to in the past, however, they must be able to apply problem solving and adaptation skills that they may never have performed before (Crawford et al., 2005).

Of course, many situations that officers encounter when responding to a call for service are straightforward in terms of the actions that are required to control the scene or subject. For these expectable or predictable situations, the procedures the officer learned during the academy and field training programs will normally give them success, so long as the officer accurately *reads the signals* of danger, recognizes the threat conditions and areas of responsibility they face, and has *practiced necessary skills* sufficiently to respond decisively.

Scrutiny Concerns

The things that weigh most heavily upon an officer are not necessarily the most important at that moment. I have heard from scores of peace officers in the aftermath of serious or lethal force incidents that at the moment they were confronted by threat their attention was focused upon the concerns they had about the scrutiny they expected to face in order to justify the amount of force they used to protect themselves or others. Their focus of attention was occupied not by the threat presented by the suspect(s); but rather by their expectations of being criticized for their actions.

Being preoccupied or distracted by concerns outside the tactical encounter greatly increases the risk of injury or error to the officer who is not mentally prepared for the encounter. As the excellent sergeant Stacy Lim of the Los Angeles Police Department stated after she survived and conquered being shot point-blank by a teenager with a .357 magnum Colt Python revolver, "Now is not the time to worry about how badly you're hurt. Now is the time to fight."

COMFORT VERSUS STRUGGLE

"Ah, I'm too tired tonight to do my scheduled workout. I feel like sitting down, watching a ball game on TV . . . and relaxing. I had a bummer of a day and just don't feel like doing it." These are thoughts and feelings that should be familiar to most people. The desire to rest, relax, and seek comfort is an instinctive, physiological and emotional reaction that returns an individual to conditions of comfort, rest, relaxation, and freedom from distress.

Peace officers can certainly choose to make themselves more comfortable by withdrawing from planned, intense physical conditioning; training; or practicing their skills. There is a damaging compromise made, however, when they do so. Their withdrawal from intense exertion has a powerful conditioning effect upon their brain. That is, they are training and conditioning their brain to submit—to surrender to distress, fatigue, or discomfort. What will they call upon when it is necessary to fight for their lives?

The brain will not do what that individual hopes it will do in a moment of crisis. Rather, it will do what he or she has trained and conditioned it to do through hundreds of repetitions of behavior. While it might sound strange to some, very often the most important times to perform an intense physical workout are when they feel like doing it the least.

Overcoming the obstacles of fatigue and discomfort through intentional acts of will and continuing aggressively in the task at hand *conditions the brain to become aggressive and energized when the officer experiences fatigue, distress, or injury* and has to fight his or her way out of trouble. This is especially important when officers are shot, stabbed, or bludgeoned.

The streets and institutions where law enforcement is performed create conditions that differ greatly from classroom and training environments. Adult education methods, or laboratory-like learning environments, while excellent in enabling officers to gain and retain information or skill just do not transfer the skills obtained effectively enough to field conditions.

Coaches of professional and amateur sports have long known of the importance of mental conditioning in their athletes' achievement of peak performance during competition. The following reference to a basketball performance at world-class levels provides an effective analogy to law enforcement work: "It is important to remember that the main task of the mental conditioning is to overcome a variety of negative factors at the beginning of the game, as well as to overcome the difficulties encountered during the game" (Rodionov, 2005).

Proficiency in the management of stress exposure in law enforcement is founded upon three overriding principles:

1. Peace officers must develop a working knowledge of, and familiarity with, the reactions that their brains and bodies undergo in response to stress-exposure conditions. They need to be shown—through their videotaped actions in realistic scenarios—how their performance is affected by precisely the same duress that they would encounter in the field. This task cannot be performed in a classroom setting or in scenarios where the officer may be able to predict (or has been told) the conditions he or she will encounter.

2. Officers must be shown how to counteract the negative effects of stress exposure at the moment they are exposed to it. They must learn to control and defuse symptoms of stress to prevent any degradation in performance, health, or family relationships.

3. All officers, especially those who do not have a great deal of prior rehearsal experience for police work, must build a great deal of self-confidence in their mastery of skills to succeed in police work. The lack of attention currently paid to mastery training in law enforcement must be changed. Peak performance is a difficult goal to attain under the best of circumstances, but the increase in self-confidence and skill that the officers achieve as they see themselves control conditions in which they initially were helpless, will be of great benefit in a wide range of work and life tasks.

WHEN PROBLEMS OCCUR

In the aftermath of investigations into an officer's actions during a crisis event, a careful police investigation will be able to reveal the errors that may have been made during a tactical encounter. It is a much more difficult task, however, to explain what took place in the officer's brain that caused those errors.

Was the officer's response driven by a conscious decision? Was the officer preoccupied or distracted by circumstances external to the tactical encounter (such as scrutiny concerns or personal issues that weighed upon his or her mind)? Or were the actions driven by the impulsive, undercontrolled internal levels of excitation triggered by the brain's reaction to threat? In that instance, officers are highly likely to engage in uncontrolled fight, flight, or freeze responses that have too often caused them to be damaged in some way.

DRIVING ON DUTY

Keith walked over to the bench we were meeting at with a pronounced limp. It was evident that, even twelve years after the accident, he continued to live in pain. "It happened on January 8, 1997," he told me. "And I had less than a year on the job when the accident happened. I was thirty-nine when I got on the job . . . working a rapid response car in the __th district. We . . . handled all the hot calls . . . armed robbery, burglar alarm, anything that was a rapid response."

He had been the passenger, since he was the junior officer. The officer who was driving had eleven years on the job. They were responding to a hot call—a report of a man with a gun in the subsidized housing projects. It had been a slow night, and all their previous calls had proven to be bogus. The call was outside of their assigned sector, but they wanted to get involved in something "hot," and so they drove to it. "We probably would have gotten yelled at and in trouble, but because of what happened to us I think they didn't say anything to us."

As a good partner, he was looking to make sure that traffic in the intersections they were passing was clear. They always wore their seat belts. There was no general order mandating that they wear the safety belts at the time, but they had reached an understanding that they would always stay as safe as they could.

"I was really surprised . . . I could see the cars," Keith told me. "There were about two or three squad cars in front of us with the blue lights going. We were in a marked squad car. And cars were actually pulling to the right out of our way. I was like, wow . . . and we're clear, clear, and when we looked up a car (in the right lane) pulls right into our lane."

He could just see the car's red brake lights flash on as the officer behind the wheel instinctively pulled their squad car out of the left or passing lane and onto a grassy median that separated the two northbound lanes from the two southbound lanes. As their vehicle went onto the median, the officer's head hit hard, either on the backrest or the window, he could not remember. He remembers being dazed when his head struck and he did not know if the officer who was driving had intended to go around the car that had cut in front of them, and then return to the roadway.

The major accident investigation team that later examined the crash scene said that the two officers were not that far from getting back on the road when their squad car struck one of the concrete planters the city had constructed to beautify the avenue they were driving on. The skid marks revealed that the officers' squad car was traveling at about sixty miles per hour, "and that's with the ABS brakes applied." The only thing that Keith remembers was an immense pressure upon his chest, which he believed was the seat belt pressing into his chest and knocking all the air from his lungs. He lost consciousness then.

Two off-duty officers from the same police department had been driving home from a movie with their wives when they saw the police car literally explode when it struck the concrete planter at high speed. An off-duty sheriff's deputy and a truck driver coming home from work saw the accident as well.

The off-duty officers and truck driver saw that the squad car was rapidly being engulfed in flames. They were afraid to move the stricken officers for fear of causing greater injury to them. However, they knew immediately that if they did not extricate the officers, they would burn to death.

They were able to open the driver's side door and remove Keith's partner from the most immediate danger. Keith was trapped, however, underneath the engine that had been pushed into the passenger compartment, the dashboard that had collapsed down upon him, and the computer console attached to the transmission hump that pushed inside the car. They pried his arms and legs loose and pulled him through the window, which saved his life. The gas tank exploded just seconds after he was pulled from the car and laid on the street. Keith referred to these individuals as "my earthly angels. Because if they just stood there and said, 'I don't want to touch him. I might f__k him up worse' . . . You know. So they got me out."

Keith's firearm had fallen back into the squad car when he was pulled through the window. Its bullets began to explode in the flames. Keith kept the completely melted firearm and showed it to me when we spoke.

It is clear that not all stress exposure conditions are unpleasant. Prior to injury, paralysis, or death in traffic collisions, most peace officers experience a euphoric charge when driving at high speed, which is often described as the "thrill of the chase."

The hunter rarely feels timid or fearful when going after the individual they are after. Indeed, a number of the paralyzed peace officers I spoke with acknowledged to me from their wheelchairs or bed that, prior to the collision that irreparably harmed them, they believed that "anyone who tells me to slow down is a coward." Until they "touch the flame" in the course of their work, many officers develop a convenient denial that "it's not going to happen to me."

One incident I shall never forget involved Antonio, a decorated narcotics enforcement officer. I was asked by his department to visit him in a hospital for neck and spine injuries following a traffic collision that left him a quadriplegic for the rest of his life.

His wife was feeding him and wiping his face. His mind was clear and alert. When I entered the room, he asked his wife to leave for a minute. Once she was outside the door, he turned to me and said, "Doc, there's nothing you have to say to me that's going to mean a f__king thing. You want to do something for me? Help me die."

He had been part of a surveillance team following a suspected Columbian bag man (the individual responsible for moving the money stashed at a drug house to a place where it can be smuggled out of the country). Countersurveillance had "burned" the officers following the car with the money. The suspect sped away and the chase was on.

Antonio was committed. This guy was not going to evade him. He crossed into oncoming traffic lanes a number of times in his attempt to get closer to the car he was chasing. When he ran head-on into a van at speeds in excess of sixty miles per hour, his life as he knew it ended. He would be dependent upon family members to feed him and clean him for the rest of his life.

At the risk of appearing as if I'm second-guessing officers' skills in handling on-duty driving responsibilities, I keep wondering: If officers took the first seconds of a high-speed pursuit, surveillance chase, or driving to a hot crime scene to *slow and control their breathing and heart rate*—to engage in purposeful, conscious self-regulation within the brain and body—how many would have been saved from the pain and death of the collisions that so often occur in enforcement driving?

And if officers, at the beginning of a high-speed foot pursuit, took that split second to confirm that the tactics they were taking and the level of their internal excitation were driven by strategic thinking and self-regulation rather than an impulsive, under-controlled action, how many would be spared the damage caused by an unanticipated ambush?

CONTINUING STRESS EXPOSURE AND THE BRAIN

Peace officers tend not to pay much attention in early parts of their career to how their brains and bodies change from exposure to the intermittent calm and crisis of law enforcement work. But the environment in which peace officers work often exerts harmful long-term problems in the form of physical and psychological changes or disturbances, physical disorders, and diseases.

Just as officers must learn how their firearm and other tools operate so that they can be used properly, they must also learn how their brain and body works under stress so that they can manage long-term or traumatic (single episode) exposure without the breakdowns that would otherwise happen.

What we do every day becomes familiar to us. Things that are familiar to us are perceived as normalcy by our brain. What becomes normal to the brain causes an adaptation that literally alters the nerve cells and pathways in the brain, changing the individual from their originally genetic "blueprints" to now-conditioned patterns of nerve and hormone response, *even when that conditioned response becomes destructive to the individual.*

Long-standing habits are comprised of neural networks or pathways. The more often a neural network organizes an event such as a memory, the more likely it is that this event will occur again and again; and when it does recur, it will take less energy to make it happen (Arden & Linford, 2009). Repeated experience of a memory increases its strength. This is the apparatus by which learning occurs.

The survival-oriented fear response that is initiated when an individual perceives threat in the environment has a downside. LeDoux (2002) showed that the amygdala, the part of the brain that activates the fear response, can be conditioned to elicit fear with nothing threatening actually being perceived by the senses. As mentioned earlier, the purposeful, executive functions of the brain (i.e., concentration, prioritizing, judging, making decisions, and regulating behaviors to meet objectives) are inhibited.

What this means is that chemical, electric, and neural changes in the body normally associated with the stress-arousal response—increased blood sugars, interruption in digestive activity, suppression of the immune system, increased heart rate, et cetera—begin to occur even when no actual emergency is occurring. Indeed, brain-imaging studies have documented significantly decreased lymphocytes (cells that battle illness) in individuals under heightened levels of stress (Axelrod & Reisine, 1984).

The majority of high-stress or crisis incidents can be expected to create an arousal or increased excitation in peace officers. However, many officers have fallen over the years due to the "flip side" of the stress response. That is, a continuing exposure to stress also entails the slowing, inhibition, and shutdown of body organs, causing illness or sudden and rapid death (Engel, 1971; Gellhorn, 1968; Gray, 1985). Furthermore, peace officers suffer physical disorder and breakdown to a significantly greater extent than do civilian workers (Blum, 1995; Violanti et al., 1988).

There are a number of contributory influences to the development of physical distress or disorder, compromise in mental activities, and emotional distress or disturbance in peace officers. Variables in the work environment, the individual's personality, and the heredity of the individual are likely contributors to the development of distress or disorder.

It is of critical importance that individual officers develop and practice proactive, intentional activities that countermand the potential for harm to them. Suggested methods and techniques to maintain effective inoculation against damage from stress exposure follow in later chapters.

There are also a number of tactical pitfalls or traps that are generated by officers' internal reactions to their exposure to heightened stress conditions. Two of the most commonly occurring ones can be described as "emotional capture" and the "approach trap."

3

EMOTIONAL CAPTURE AND THE APPROACH TRAP

EMOTIONAL CAPTURE

"I am a law enforcement officer. I gave you a legal and proper command, and you are refusing to comply with that command. People need to do what I tell them to do. I enforce the law. You are now facing a 'contempt of cop' situation because you are righteously pissing me off."

These are some of the moments where the actions of a non-compliant or aggressive subject create anger in the peace officers that have to deal with them. An officer's anger or some other, uncontrolled excitation surge or urgency—whether they are aware of it or not—can substantially alter and disrupt their work performance.

For example, when someone the officer is attempting to detain suddenly runs from him or her, that officer's immediate reaction is most likely to take the form of a compelling impulse to run after the suspect individual. It is often difficult for peace officers to assess and control the possible consequences of a course of action they begin to take when the thrill of the chase or a surge of anger captures them.

The conscious mental activity they should be engaged in—to read the conditions of the scene, to prioritize the responsibilities they have to deal with first, and to place themselves in and maintain positions of advantage—is lessened or extinguished by their strong drive to close in on and overcome the suspect.

The thrill of the chase produces a euphoric feeling in peace officers. After all, the closer you get to a suspect and the quicker you get there, the faster you'll take control of them . . . right? Well, yes, most of the time that is true. It is not, however, always true.

"DON'T ARGUE WITH ME. YOU WILL DO WHAT YOU'RE TOLD!"

Paul was almost finished with the last shift of his workweek. He normally rode a motorcycle as a traffic officer, but was working in a patrol vehicle that night due to inclement weather. He had fourteen years of experience as a peace officer.

Paul had originally worked at another police agency where he specialized in narcotics enforcement before he resigned there to work at the department that was much closer to his home and had a work schedule that would allow him to spend more time with his family.

He had been a good-natured person in the first several years of his work at the new department, with an easy laugh and quick-witted sense of humor. He was well liked and respected as a "stand-up, squared-away cop" by other officers and supervisors of his department. He did his job without complaint, and was always ready to lend a hand when someone needed help. He was nominated for selection to the department's combined crime impact and SWAT team, an honor of which he was proud.

In addition to the training for SWAT, Paul trained and competed as a heavyweight powerlifter. He pushed major weight around in the gym. His trapezius muscles were so enlarged that he appeared not to have a neck. He consistently won or placed well in Police Olympics competitions, and was confident about the strength and power he possessed. He had never lost a physical struggle in his fourteen years as a peace officer.

His personality began to change during the eleventh year of his law enforcement career. While he had always shown a patient, easygoing demeanor toward difficult people in the past, he began to become easily frustrated and was likely to lose his temper whenever someone argued with him or questioned commands he gave them.

People started filing complaints alleging that Paul had demonstrated an angry, intimidating demeanor when they asked him a question or tried to explain something they were doing. According to many of the complaints about Paul's demeanor, his response to their questions or attempts to explain their actions was the same, angry comment: "Don't argue with me! You will do as you are told!"

More telling, perhaps, was the increased number of questionable uses of force he engaged in during situations that he had managed in the past without needing to put his hands or taser on anyone.

Because he was a well-respected officer, and because cops are usually reluctant to confront personal "quirks" in each other, no one in the department spoke to him about the alteration observed in his personality. The fact that he demonstrated moodiness, irritability, and "short-fused," angry reactions to things he used to laugh about were discussed by his co-workers and supervisors, but never with him.

What no one at his department knew was that Paul and his wife had been having serious, intransigent problems in their relationship. They had begun to argue and fight much more than they ever did in the early years of their marriage. Their problems came to a head when Paul came home from his normal work shift unexpectedly early one night, and found his wife sitting at their dining room table having a glass of wine with a police officer they had socialized with a number of times along with the visiting officer's own wife. Paul's wife swore up and down that nothing wrong or illicit had happened, and that she had not betrayed him. She yelled that Paul had stopped talking to her, and she had just reached out to their mutual friend for someone to listen to her.

Paul stared at her in shock and disbelief. His first impulse was to shoot them both. Instead, he turned, and without saying a word, walked out of his house. He felt humiliated. He never spoke a word to anyone about the feelings that had started to burn holes inside of him.

Paul found it hard to believe his wife's protestations that she hadn't cheated on him. He felt betrayed by the one person he figured he would always be able to trust. After an ugly argument one night turned into name-calling and hysteria, Paul decided that he couldn't take it anymore and moved out of his house. He was experiencing a sickening combination of grief over what he believed was the loss of his home and family, as well as feelings of rage that never seemed to diminish or go away no matter how many times they were released in the gym or at someone who was talking back or acting like a jerk to him.

First and foremost, Paul knew that his three young children had to be the priority in anything he did. After a number of weeks away from his home and family, he felt it necessary to try to accept his wife's continuing apologies for hurting him and her continued statements that she had not had sex with the other officer. He agreed to her requests for him to come back home so that they could work at putting their marriage back on track. They began to see a therapist. But like many cops, he remained suspicious of his wife's activities and the feelings with which he was struggling did not go away.

Everything he saw looked dirty and soiled to him. When other officers teased him about how popular he was becoming with the driving public, he was quick to take offense. His guts were on fire, but he was just not going to talk about it to anyone. He withdrew from his friends, greatly increased the amounts of alcohol he was drinking alone, and stopped doing the things he had enjoyed in the past. His hangovers prevented his usual commitment to his strength and physical-conditioning efforts.

The traffic lieutenant called Paul into his office at the beginning of his duty watch one night and counseled him that the courtesy complaints he was getting could cause him and the department unnecessary stress. He told Paul that a number of his fellow officers had expressed concern for him. Without divulging any of the things that had been bothering him, Paul assured the lieutenant he would watch his demeanor with people, and try to avoid getting pissed off as quickly as he had been.

He was working that same night on a drunk driver detail when he saw a late-model car weaving back and forth across the centerline of the street. He called in to dispatch that he was stopping a possible DUI suspect, and gave his location. He turned on his overhead lights and went after the vehicle, which continued to move slowly for over half a block before pulling to the side of the street and stopping. As he reached the driver's side front window, he could already smell the strong odor of alcohol wafting up at him.

The driver looked up at him with bleary, bloodshot, and unfocused eyes. Paul asked the driver to "please get out of the car, sir." The driver's response to Paul's request was to emphatically shake his head from side to side, saying, "Nope. I don't need to get out of the car. We can talk right here where we are."

Paul again ordered the driver to get out of his car, with much greater intensity this time. He was getting angry and did not want to take any guff from this intoxicated jerk. He didn't need the aggravation, especially today, just after the lieutenant had basically warned him to watch himself. The driver told him, "I'm not getting out of this car. You go get backup and I'll wait here for you."

Paul yelled at him: "I don't need f___king backup for you, asshole!" He opened the door and started to pull the driver out of the car, but he had very little leverage in the tug-of-war that had now begun.

After several moments of struggle, and with a strong pull, the man leaned back, causing Paul to lose his balance and fall into the car on top of him. They were now chest-to-chest. Paul was stuck between the steering wheel and the seat back. He felt movement underneath him, and saw that the driver was thrusting his hand down into the seat. "Oh, that's what's happening," he thought. "He's got dope that he doesn't want me to find."

Paul tried to get to his feet. He began to talk now to the driver, trying to de-escalate the situation and get him to stop struggling. "Stop resisting," he said. "No one has to get hurt here. Stop fighting."

Expecting to see the driver come out with dope in his hand, Paul never saw the gun that the intoxicated man pulled out. Suddenly, there was the muzzle pointing straight at him. As Paul struggled to get out of the car, he heard popping sounds that sounded like firecrackers going off. He felt the first two bullets strike him on the front of his bulletproof vest. The third bullet struck him in the throat. It traversed the side of his jaw and snipped a sliver of tissue from his carotid artery before it lodged in his brachial plexus. As he turned to his right, recoiling from the gunfire he was taking, the fourth and fifth bullets struck Paul in his left arm and hand. He knew that he had to fight back or he was going to die. He had to stop this guy from shooting him.

Without being conscious that he was doing so, Paul pulled his gun from its holster and returned fire. He wasn't aiming so much as he was trying to get the man to stop shooting. Although he did not know it at the time, the first bullets Paul fired into the car were fatal to the man who had tried to murder him.

A resident who lived across the street from where the shooting occurred heard the gunshots, looked out, and saw a police officer falling to the ground. He then saw someone sprawled across the front seat of the car with his feet sticking out. He immediately called 9-1-1 and told them, "One of your officers just got shot. He's fallen down on the ground. You'd better get here quick." He gave his address and stayed on the phone as requested by the dispatch operator so that he could help guide other officers to the location without delay. He was urged to keep his distance from the vehicle, because there were many pissed-off cops coming to the scene as fast as they could, and the dispatcher told him that she didn't want these officers mistaking him for a bad guy.

Backup now began to come from all over the city and county to help, although at this point they did not know that the victim officer was Paul. The dispatcher requested a roll call from all officers in the field as they were driving to the location of the shooting. Everyone but Paul responded.

Paul couldn't move or speak. When the third bullet struck him, he had fallen to the ground as blood poured out of his mouth. The trauma of the gunshot wound had caused his airways to swell up with blood and inflammation, to the point that he could not get enough air to breathe.

He found that by making grunting and coughing sounds deep in his throat, he could create an airway to take in life-giving air. He believed that he was going to watch himself bleed out and die while he listened to the sound of the sirens coming closer to him.

The next sounds Paul heard were of tires squealing and doors slamming. The first face he saw was that of his best friend in the department. He whispered to his buddy and asked him to tell his wife and kids that he loved them. The responding officer, through tears that were flowing down his face, told Paul to "shut the f__k up, stupid. You're going to tell them yourself. You're not going to die. Stay with me, Paulie. Don't close your eyes!"

His buddy's words were a great comfort to him and Paul started to believe that maybe it was true—maybe he was not going to die. His spirits rose again later, at the hospital, after the head surgeon told Paul that the size and strength of the muscles in his jaw and neck were what had saved his life by causing the bullet to veer to the side instead of continuing on its path and severing his brain stem.

The doctors had performed a tracheotomy to provide Paul with an airway, because the severe swelling in his neck prevented them from putting an air tube down his throat at the beginning of surgery. After three surgeries, he had to communicate through writing notes. Paul spent three weeks recuperating in the hospital after being transferred out of the Intensive Care Unit.

After two weeks, the doctors closed the hole they had cut with the tracheotomy, and Paul was able to breathe and speak much more easily. As soon as he was cleared to do so, and in spite of the severe pain he experienced constantly, he started to lift small weights to help in his struggle to get back to the person he was before he was shot.

There were additional wounds, however, less easily observable, that created significant obstacles to his recovery. Paul could not point to them in order to explain what had happened to his sense of himself as a cop and as a man because these wounds were not visible. He had lost the confidence that once came to him automatically.

No matter how many days and weeks went by, Paul continued to experience intrusive memories of the muzzle flash he saw as he was shot in the face. He had experienced a profound feeling of helplessness when he collapsed on the ground and could no longer do anything to fight back. He had never felt anything like this in his life. He was totally unable to control the fear he felt at the memory, and lost a great deal of self-esteem in the process.

In addition, and no matter how many times it was pointed out to him, he had no recollection or awareness of how courageously he had fought back at the moment he saw that he was being attacked. Instead, all he remembered of the shooting was his immobility and helplessness—the evidence of his failure and defeat—and the belief that he was going to die.

The reason why Paul was having such a tough time dealing with the distress and loss of confidence has a great deal to do with the tendency of peace officers to ignore, distance, or detach themselves from troubling or troublesome emotional activity at the earliest parts of their careers. This conditioning occurs because there are high levels of *social desirability* and *social pressure* to do so. The unwritten law prohibiting shows of emotion (except, of course, acceptable feelings like anger or contempt for the jerks of the world) is simple: "If you feel, you cry. If you cry, you've lost control. If you lose control, you can't be a cop."

When officers are severely wounded or injured, however, or are psychologically traumatized by an incident—that is, when they've lost their sense of the person they were prior to being struck—their strategy of distancing themselves consciously from their inner turmoil only makes them less aware of how to deal with the problems they face effectively.

Following his release from the hospital, and continuing for months afterwards once he returned to work, Paul went through a great deal of anxiety whenever he faced an unknown condition or when he felt a potential threat or obstacle to feeling in control of events. The feelings of helplessness he had experienced at the moment when he was shot had been "burned" or "super-conditioned" into his memory.

No matter how much effort he expended to keep his memories of being shot from consciousness, he had no idea how to stop them. He continued to re-experience feelings of helplessness and defeat that now seemed a constant companion in everything he did.

Paul returned to active duty within five months of the shooting, well before anyone had expected him to and before his doctors wanted him to. The person who returned to work, however, had been changed. Few people in law enforcement—and almost no one in society—can appreciate the difficulty that wounded or injured officers experience in their efforts to regain their "edge," that feeling of confidence that they will be victorious in whatever difficulty they face. The road back is long and arduous.

Paul had never been much of a worrier. But he now second-guessed everything he attempted. Difficulties in his marriage became more severe as his wife told him that he was different than the person she had chosen to marry. She pointed out the fact that they never did anything that was fun anymore, and all he seemed to want to do was to sit at home and anesthetize himself with alcohol. She told him that he was like a stranger to her now, and had stopped letting her know anything that he was feeling.

Paul could not really argue these points, because he felt like a stranger to himself as well. They eventually divorced. The ending of his marriage was apparently the "kick in the pants" he needed to deal realistically with his physical pain, his poor self-image and self-esteem, and the emotions that caused him continuing distress.

For the first time since he was shot, he talked about feelings that he would never have imagined talking about. He worked hard to "make peace" with his memories of the shooting and, more importantly, acknowledged the fact that it was his "short fuse" that resulted in him taking the actions with the resistant driver that he would not have done were he in control of his emotions. He realized that his anger had robbed him of the patience and problem-solving skills that had helped him so many times in defusing potentially explosive encounters with difficult or disturbed people.

Emotional capture is a term that is only sometimes discussed in law enforcement training. However, the "fire flaming in the gut"—the surge of internal excitation, or feelings of anger—can sabotage an officer's ability to organize and regulate their actions in response to a crisis or threat.

Over the years many people in law enforcement have scoffed at the idea that a peace officer would not be in control of his or her emotions. The idea that an officer would not be capable of "keeping in" whatever he or she felt meant to many in the field that this individual did not belong in law enforcement. It was believed that emotions should be ignored or blocked, "stuffed down," so that no overt disclosure—or awareness of them—would occur. Neither attention nor effort was spent to educate or train incoming and advanced officers in how to control their brain, body, and behavioral response during high levels of stress exposure. The result of this avoidance has been damage and death to those who served that never needed to happen.

Emotional capture means that a resistant individual's curses and yelling at him or her, for example, or the act of someone running from them create intense and powerful drives that can easily take primacy over his or her use of judgment. That is, when "capture" occurs, it is an emotional drive that is determining the course of actions these individuals take, not a strategic plan that enables them to organize and control their response.

Another condition that has resulted in a great deal of harm to peace officers is referred to as *the approach trap*. It describes the compulsion or urgency to get close to someone, at times when tactical propriety and their safety require a more careful approach.

THE APPROACH TRAP: "GO IN THERE AND GET THIS GUY TAKEN CARE OF"

On the day he was shot, Max had taken his daughters swimming at the YMCA. It was a great day, just experiencing father-daughter happiness. "It was a great afternoon . . . You know, [his three-and-a-half-year-old daughter] jumping off the diving board. Showing off for her father. The other one was one and a half." That was the last good day he had with his children.

It was hot when Max dressed for work that night. The district he worked in was the slowest in the city and, as he did with other nights at work, he expected that this shift would be a quiet one. It was the summer of 1988 in a large Midwestern city. He and his partner worked a plainclothes tactical assignment, and both had several years of skilled and successful police experience. Pursuant to their tradition, they decided to start their shift at a local submarine sandwich shop.

They had just begun to eat their meal when a call came of a mother-son domestic disturbance. The reporting party was the mother, who expressed a need for help with her mentally disturbed son. Dispatch gave the call to a uniformed patrol unit. Max and his partner were not seated far from the address broadcast. They looked at each other and said, "Let's go to the disturbance call. We'll get the arrest we're supposed to get for the night, and then coast for the rest of the shift."

The officers in uniform loved it when plainclothes tactical officers took the first arrest, because it freed them from spending the first hours of their shift doing paperwork. Max notified dispatch that they would respond to assist the uniformed officers. They arrived at the location first.

An elderly woman was standing in front of the house. She was pointing into the house and kept repeating the same two words in broken English: "He crazy! He crazy! He crazy!" The officers asked her if there were any weapons in the house, or anything else that they should be concerned about, but all they could get from her were the same, repeated words: "He crazy! He crazy!"

Max told the woman, "Okay, we'll take care of it." He told his partner to take the rear door "in case stupid runs out the back." His response tendencies and expectations of what he would encounter in this type of incident were based upon his past experiences with mentally disturbed people: such as "Buddy, I don't want to hear your story. Ma says you're nuts." All he thought about was his desire to put this guy in handcuffs and not waste any more time with someone who would wind up going to a hospital anyway. "We want to go look for burglars." His attitude was along the lines of, "Tell it to the judge, not me"—and then, "Mom, what happened? Okay, here you go, sign this complaint and we're out of here."

The first thing that captured Max's attention when he entered the residence was the sign handwritten either with lipstick or some type of liquid marker over the entire wall: "You will free me or else; and quit going through my stuff."

Oh, this isn't good, thought Max. The woman's statement "He crazy" seemed to be an accurate description after all.

All of a sudden, things were not so calm anymore. Max drew his gun and kept it pointed down along his leg. "I'm thinking, 'Okay, we're going to be rocking and rolling. This is going to be a fight.' Just by looking at what's here. He just told me, 'I'm nuts.'"

The house he and the two uniformed officers entered was a small one. The front door opened into a narrow hallway. They entered a front room that led to the kitchen at the right side of the room. He heard the subject say, "Get out of my house." Max answered, "Hey pal, we're just here to talk to you. That's all we want to do."

The sound of the subject's voice came from the kitchen but Max could not see him from the front room. He thought then about human nature: "He's going to be sitting at the table having a beer, having something—you know, 'get out of my house'—something like that. The fact is, though, he was crouched down behind the stove. And you couldn't see him."

Max felt compelled to locate where the mentally disturbed person was. He entered the kitchen at the right side just in front of the open doorway. He visualized in his mind's eye that he would observe a male having a beer, seated at the dining table, the corner of which he had seen across the kitchen from the open doorway. The position he took against the wall at the doorway to the kitchen would have been to his advantage had this expectation been accurate.

"You couldn't see him. . . . I go to look over expecting to see him over there. He was crouched down behind the stove. He just jumped up—boom—got me. Got me with a .380. I go down on my back like a ton of bricks. And I'm trying to kill him. But I was like instantly paralyzed. I'm lying there in the hallway on my back. He's in the kitchen. The two uniforms retreat to the front. And I'm lying there with a gun battle going on over my head."

After the two uniform officers withdrew from the kitchen, Max's partner appeared and put out the broadcast that there was an officer down. The remainder of his eight-member tactical team arrived shortly thereafter. Speaking was difficult for Max because the bullet had entered the trachea.

The other officers were lifting him up. He spoke in a whisper because air was hissing out of the hole in his throat. He told them, "Take me outside to die. Don't let me die in this asshole's house. Tell ____ and the girls I love them." Everything went dark then.

Max regained consciousness three days later in the Intensive Care Unit of the hospital. His wife was seated at the side of his bed. He made writing motions with his hands and, when paper and pen was given to him, wrote, "Bad guy?" He was told then that a standoff had occurred. An entry team had been preparing to go in hard and fast. They were given the green light, according to the following reasoning: "If he won't give up you are to shoot the suspect and keep shooting until he stops moving. He just shot a police officer." They deployed tear gas into the kitchen prior to entering and then heard the gunshot with which the subject took his own life.

Max had several life-threatening medical episodes even up to four years after this incident, where his life had to be saved all over again. The first one occurred a month following the shooting, when he suffered a pulmonary embolism. His throat was opened in surgery and his lungs filled with blood. He started to drown in his own body fluids. One week after that a car was sent to pick up his wife with the message that he would die that night. The medical term was "adult respiratory distress," a complication created by his smoking two packs of cigarettes a day from the time he was a teenager. The surgeons broke his ribs so that they could attempt to remove the residue of smoking from his lungs in an effort to save him. He was in the hospital for four months.

Seven months after he was shot, Max developed ulcerative colitis, a condition that often accompanies severe trauma to the body. He had maintained his upper body strength, but during the rehabilitation process, he had to learn to use his legs again.. He maintained a strong will to handle his new situation as best he could: "If this is the cards I got, so be it. I'll make the necessary arrangements at the house. But I'm going to survive."

The hardest part of Max's recovery came after the medical crises had lessened. He was constantly agitated. He could no longer relax no matter where he was or what he did. He couldn't control the fear and helplessness inside of him. He became the passenger in his car, which was now driven by his wife. He had canes and braces for both legs. He kept a .45 automatic stuck between his legs.

He was fearful to the point of terror that someone was going to walk up to his car and shoot him. He had premonitions about being attacked no matter how safe an environment he was in. With the firearm in his lap, he remained in a hypervigilant condition, ready to shoot whomever walked up to his car.

His wife would begin crying during his premonitions. She begged him: "You need help. You've got to talk to somebody." It was difficult for him to put into words how helpless he felt since being shot. All the confidence he had felt as an elite tactical officer was gone.

A turning point in Max's recovery arrived in the form of a visit from a lieutenant who accompanied the department chaplain to his bedside. The lieutenant had been one of thirteen Chicago police officers who were shot on the same day by a sniper. The lieutenant, who had been a young patrol officer at the time, was kept in the hospital for one year. During that time he'd had to wear the apparatus feared and disliked by officers recovering from core-area organ wounds: a colostomy bag.

Max started thinking differently from that moment on: "God, this guy's here and not selling me some bill of goods about not making it back. He made it. If he can do it, I'm going to do it." Max never looked back from that point. He came to realize, especially concerning his wife and daughters, that there was a reason he survived.

He had to cope with the anger he directed at the suspect, and the anger he felt toward himself: "How could I have allowed myself to get shot? What did I do wrong? I'm better than the average officer. I took so much pride and so much care." He preached to other officers all the time: "Let's be careful, guys. Let's back up each other." It took two full years for him to feel good about his life again.

What happened to Max is a fairly classic example of a totally unexpected assault on a peace officer. An academy instructor approached Max two years later and stated that he wanted to re-create his shooting incident as a training tool. They set up a room with the same floor plan as was in the house, with a role-player performing the same acts as the suspect. All recruits went through the same scenario. Every recruit was shot.

Does this mean that the scenario was unwinnable? A number of experienced officers I approached with this incident believed that officers would not be able to prevent themselves from being shot because, "You don't expect someone to be hiding behind the stove."

The belief that officers would be unable to react quickly enough to prevent themselves from being shot is based to a large extent in how veteran officers have been "captured" by their habitual ways of approaching and controlling disturbed persons. Their regular thinking is, "Go in there and get this guy taken care of." Once they enter the room where the suspect lies in wait, they cannot take it back and ask for a do-over.

To avoid the traps you can't get out of, you must avoid creating expectations: that is, predictions about what you're going to find. The "Oh, it's going to be one of these" because it had always gone that way before must be extinguished as a habit—one that is used by too many peace officers.

Having expectations about what the contact is going to be like makes you feel less anxiety, but also sets you up for surprise, startle, and shock. The reality is that some ambushes will occur solely because officers place themselves in danger when they base their approach and tactical plan upon what they expect to happen—and not upon what they actually see and read *then-and-there* at a scene.

When their predictions turn out *not* to be accurate, they are delayed for just a split second by surprise or startle. It is in this moment that officers are successfully attacked. Unfortunately, only in a relatively small percentage of law enforcement agencies is attention paid in law enforcement training specifically for adaptation expertise—proficiency in shifting one's approach, mind-set, thinking, perceptions, and tactics in real time—without shock or delay—to respond effectively and decisively to unexpected threat conditions. For adaptation proficiency to be developed, it is the mind and psychology of the individual officer must be trained, rather than the tactics they used to resolve some scenario-based situation being evaluated.

I asked Max if, now that he had lived with his wounds and recovery for so long, there was anything he might have done differently that would have changed the outcome. "I would never have gone into that kitchen," he replied. "I would have stood back and called for SWAT to do their thing."

Prior to and during his assignment as a tactical officer, Max had developed habitual ways of performing his duties. He had experienced success after success by closing in on subjects and suspects as quickly as possible and taking command by seizing control.

He did not feel the need to take the time to slow down and confirm that the tactics he was about to use were the most effective and safe given the circumstances he encountered—he never had to before. No trainer or mentor had cautioned him that the very successes he achieved by performing in the ways that he did often blinds officers to the fact that working on "automatic pilot" can (and often does) create extreme danger for them.

Obviously, approaching and closing in on a potentially dangerous or flee-ing individual and gaining control of them are most often the greatest ben-efit to peace officers, as it permits them to seize initiative. But that action needs to be a purposeful decision, not an impulsive action driven by a surge of internal excitation or feeling of urgency, and not simply due to habits because "it always worked this way before."

It wouldn't make any sense to imagine a peace officer giving away the advantages in a tactical encounter that training and discipline are supposed to provide them. Peace officers already start their enforcement response after a suspect "calls the play." Why give anyone further ammunition? At the moment of an unexpected crisis, however, even expert peace officers can react to the stress to which they are exposed with actions based not upon a strategy or plan they had intentionally worked out, but rather with actions driven by habit, or by some instinctive urge or discharge of excitation that places them in lethal situations they never expected and for which they are not prepared.

IMAGE, EXPECTATIONS, AND PRE-JUDGMENT

Nick was a veteran police officer with eleven years of law enforcement expe-rience, working as a "canine officer." He was well respected by his co-work-ers and supervisors. He and Otto, his canine partner, were patrolling their city during a late summer heat wave.

They were inching along in the midst of rush-hour traffic when Nick observed an adult male Caucasian on a side street moving rapidly toward the main thoroughfare. He was dressed in a white dress shirt, tie, and a suit vest and pants. The man was gesturing to Nick in a manner that suggested he was asking for help. Nick at first thought that the man might have been the victim of a robbery or mugging.

The man did not stop at the sidewalk, but entered the street to the rear of Nick's vehicle. Nick now was concerned that "this guy probably just got robbed, and now he's going to get himself hit by a car." The man appeared to Nick as a tax-paying, working person—not the look of a dope fiend, parolee, or gang member that would activate Nick's "danger signals."

"Stay back!" Nick yelled to the man. "Stay on the sidewalk, damn it. You're going to get hit."

The man continued to approach the canine unit in an apparent state of agitation or upset. His face was tightened into a grimace, as if he was in pain.

Otto was now in a frenzy. He was barking, growling, and clawing at the window to get at the approaching man. Now Nick was preoccupied not only with his expectation that the man would be hit by a car, but also with his fear that the man would get up close to the vehicle and be bitten by Otto. "Stay away from this car," Nick yelled. "There's a dangerous dog in the car!" The man did not slow or stop his approach.

He was now rounding the rear of Nick's police vehicle to get to the driver's side. *Damn it!* thought Nick. *Now he's going to get both of us run over.* He opened the driver's door in a hurry and got out to face the man and get him safely to the curb. It was then that he saw the "doll's-eye stare," facial grimaces, and spastic movement in the man's face. It became clear too late that this man was "dusted," or under the influence of a Phencyclidine-like drug (e.g., PCP—also called "Angel Dust"—or Ketamine, an animal tranquilizer). Nick's expectations about the man's characteristics had been wrong.

The man came at Nick without slowing down and grabbed him around his body, pushing him backward and down. Nick staggered a few steps and then tripped and fell. The man was making growling sounds like a rabid animal.

The man's strength overwhelmed Nick. He was unable to push the man off him. The man released the hold he had Nick in and began to strike him with one hand while he reached for Nick's firearm with the other.

Nick knew now that he was fighting for his life. The two of them struggled for control of the weapon. The man had his hand on the barrel. Nick fought to turn the muzzle toward the man.

The sound of the weapon firing was muffled in between their two bodies. Nick said, "I felt like someone stabbed a hot poker into my leg. I saw smoke coming off my leg." The man let go of the barrel when the gun went off, and Nick was able to move his hand to the mechanism that opened the rear door of his canine vehicle and push it.

Otto exploded out of the car and took the man by his upper arm. The dog was a large Czech shepherd, weighing close to one hundred pounds. His snarls and growling sounded to Nick "like a beautiful beast from hell." Otto's attack and hold took the man off Nick, but he then picked Otto up and slammed him onto the pavement, fracturing two vertebrae.

The man again came at Nick, who fired several bullets into the man's body before he finally stopped and fell to the ground. Nick then called for help. "Shots fired! Shots fired! Officer down! Roll Paramedics Code Three! Officer down!"

An off-duty police officer who had been driving through the area heard the commotion and came to help Nick. He placed the downed attacker at gunpoint while Nick tried to comfort Otto.

Nick became aware that blood was soaking his pant leg. He saw the pool that was starting to form, and he realized that the bullet had probably cut an artery. Several police and sheriff's vehicles arrived then. A deputy sheriff ran up to Nick and placed his hands around Nick's thigh, putting pressure on the pulsing bullet wound. The deputy's action may well have saved Nick's life. Without it, he could well have gone into shock from blood loss and died.

In addition to the physical wound he had to recover from to get back to work, Nick was greatly troubled by two conditions. While he didn't tell his fellow officers, he had believed that he was about to be killed at the moment when the deranged man physically overpowered him and put his hand on Nick's gun.

In addition, he was dismayed at how badly he had misperceived the actions of his assailant. His self-confidence and self-esteem had been founded upon his ability to "read" people and stay ahead of the curve. He thought he would exit his vehicle and help a guy who looked like a victim. He was mortified at how wrong his expectations had been. I have come to perceive officers' pre-judging an impending law enforcement contact as akin to walking into quicksand.

How often have peace officers experienced the feeling of great relief— and an "Oh, shit!" feeling—when they realize that they have unwittingly placed themselves in a highly vulnerable spot; and, but for the grace of God, they could have been killed? They allowed the "charge," frustration, impatience, or urgency to close in on someone to take primacy in their brains—overcoming and inhibiting the thinking and reasoning parts of their brain that would identify to them that they were placing themselves in great danger. Or the officers had formed expectations that, when proven incorrect, had slowed their response enough for them to be harmed. They were unable to immediately *act upon* the threat because they were first *reacting to* it.

It takes great courage to face the faults that we possess in our use of judgment, our biases and habits, and our personality characteristics that predispose us to respond in a certain way, with enough honesty to realize that we may need to change our perspective, thinking, and approach to how we work and live.

The willingness to honestly view self-defeating habits in oneself and be open to corrective input is a cornerstone of effective tactical planning and action. These are simple lessons to learn as a preventive activity.

4

GIVING AWAY THE ADVANTAGE

GIVING AWAY THE ADVANTAGE

Stan was the new guy in the narcotics enforcement unit. He had just been accepted to the specialized detail, but had eight years of previous police experience. He had worked patrol, and also had been a plainclothes tactical officer assigned to the public housing projects.

The sergeant of the team to which he was to report was on furlough, so he was being bounced from team to team before being permanently assigned to a squad. On October 5, 1994, he was told to meet other officers in a local precinct's parking lot prior to serving a search warrant on a suspected drug dealer. Stan was very happy about this because he would finally be working with his own team. It was a beautiful day.

Five officers met in the parking lot. When Stan had served one of the many high-risk warrants while working as a tactical officer in the projects, there were always eight plainclothes officers and at least one marked unit with two uniformed officers. He explained, "And we always had a briefing as far as how many exits there were. Who did we expect to be in there? Were there any kids? We didn't want to knock a door down and kill a kid. We worried about dogs, stuff like that. We had those briefings all the time, and if anybody ever had a bad feeling, we wouldn't do it. And that's all it would take."

This time, though, the number of officers assigned to the search warrant was much smaller. In addition to Stan, there was one sergeant, the officer he drove with, the officer whose warrant it was, and a female officer. I asked Stan if he thought anything at the time about the fact that there were only five officers for the warrant service. He acknowledged that it certainly did cross his mind. He felt uneasy but, being the "new guy," he didn't want to create problems.

He told me that he was "pretty much told, 'Hey . . . you go be the hammer,'" meaning it would be Stan's job to take down the front door of the suspect's apartment. "And I felt good about that because I wasn't being stuck at the back door—you're a new guy, you don't want to be stuck at the back door. You want to be where the action is."

Though he was glad to be part of the action, Stan still felt uneasy. The briefing consisted only of a statement by the investigating officer that the suspect was known to carry two nine-millimeter handguns and that it was a drug warrant they were serving. Stan got in the car with the other officer and asked him, "What's going on? I don't even know where the hell we're going." The other officer didn't know, either.

Stan began to mention his concern about how little briefing they had been given and how few officers were working the warrant service. "I didn't want to cause too many waves. But I was, like, 'What's going on here?'" This action just did not feel right to him.

The other officer began to explain the history of competition among the different teams that made up the narcotics bureau in their city. The office they all worked in consisted of semi-private cubicles where conversations could be overheard. There had been a team discussing a search warrant in one of their cubicles. Someone in the next cubicle heard where they were going, and those officers got in their cars and hit the building the other team had been discussing. So now everything had become top secret. The officer told Stan, "Nobody wants to say anything until you're there."

The team gathered in the parking lot behind a two-story apartment complex. Stan carried the hammer that would be used to breach the door. The sergeant led the way, running down a pathway into the housing complex. Just behind him were the officer whose case this was, followed by Stan, the officer he drove with, and the third, female officer. The female officer was assigned to the rear of the complex, and the four other officers were placed at the front door. They still did not know the layout of the residence.

The sergeant opened the screen and banged his open hand several times on the door, announcing, "Police! Search warrant!" Stan's adrenaline levels were sky high, "because you just get that way when you're the hammer guy." At a nod from the sergeant, Stan hit the door. It did not budge. It was a fortified door, made of steel.

Stan hit the door with the hammer fifteen to twenty times and wound up pulling the steel frame out of the mortar around the door. He then saw that a two-by-four piece of wood had been braced along the door and bolted into the doorframe. He figured that the suspect had either never used that front door, or else had recently fortified it. He then handed the hammer to the officer he'd driven there with and that officer began to hammer at the door.

The two-by-four began to loosen as they kept working on opening the door. It was at this point that "all hell broke loose." Stan's car partner was turning to hand the hammer back to him so that he could continue hitting the door. At this point, Stan didn't think that anyone was at home. He hadn't heard any sounds from behind the door.

As he was reaching to receive the hammer, the officer behind him—the one who had initiated the warrant—could not wait any longer. He said, "f___k this" and knocked Stan to the side. He ran to the front door and pulled himself over the loosened two-by-four and into the apartment.

"It happened so quick," Stan recalled. "I turned to the sergeant and was going to say, 'What the f__k did he just do?' And all of a sudden I hear, 'boom.'"

Stan had been in the military and had been a police officer for eight years. He knew that gunshots were going off inside the apartment. He thought then, *We're in a world of trouble now.* The door was not sufficiently opened for them all to get inside.

He felt an extreme urgency to get inside that apartment to protect the officer who had gone inside. He took a step forward to grab the hammer from the officer who was holding it. However, he told me, "That officer threw the hammer to the ground and ran back in the direction they had come. He kept running."

There were three more shots fired, not quite as loud as the first. The sergeant was yelling to the officer inside, asking him if he had been hit. That officer answered yes. Using the door for cover, the sergeant began to kick at it, but it would not budge. Stan didn't know what the sergeant could see inside of the apartment—the opening was still too narrow to lean one's whole body through. The sergeant yelled to the officer to stay in the kitchen: "We'll get you out. Don't worry, we'll get you out."

Stan was thinking about the suspect, "Okay, he shot a cop; he's going to go out the back door. He's going to kill that female police officer that's back there." He began to run around the apartment complex to help her, but then he heard "a whole bunch of shots fired in the gun battle going on between the cops and the suspect at that front door." Stan turned and ran back to try and get through the front door again.

Stan's mind was racing: "I just got tunnel vision on the door and I said if I run fast enough and hard enough, I could knock that door down, get the guy that's in there, drag him out, and let the other cops deal with this guy." Stan was about fifteen feet away from the front door when he got shot in the face. Out of the corner of his eye he saw glass exploding from a side window and puffs of smoke coming out of it.

"Now it hits me that the crook is shooting right from this window . . . and I start to crouch and bring my Beretta (semi-automatic firearm) around my body. As I'm doing this I'm looking into the window. But I can't see anything because he's got heavy drapes. I'm pretty close to pulling the trigger and I actually was able to think that if I fire into that window I might hit the officer inside and that would defeat the whole purpose. But I also said, 'I can't stop here . . . I've got to go forward. I need to get through that door.'"

Stan was hit a second time. The bullet went through his arm and across his vest. The sergeant was turning to see what was going on behind him when Stan slammed into him. "I hit him so hard that we both now are knocked into the doorway . . . he's laying on the two-by-four and I'm on top of him. We're pinned in between this doorway. So, you know that saying, 'You never hear the one that gets you'? This guy was still firing out of that window. I think at the time I was trying to process, What's my next move? Do I run into this apartment now?"

Stan told me that he felt the third shot hit him before he heard it. He got hit just below his vest. The bullet went through his right kidney, his colon, liver, diaphragm, and lung. It exited through his shoulder. He described his reaction to this wound as the spring of a clock breaking internally. He thought at that time, "I'm going to die in a f___king Southside apartment and I'm never going to see my family again." He was slipping into shock.

Stan had lived with his grandmother when he was a young child. He suddenly saw himself playing on the floor of his grandmother's basement apartment. His attention was drawn back to the present as he heard the sergeant yelling at him to get off of him. "This guy's going to come in here and kill us both! Get the f__k off of me!"

While Stan believed that he was dying, he knew that he didn't want to take the sergeant with him. He pushed himself off the sergeant, who now saw that the shots were coming from the window and started firing at it.

Badly wounded, Stan wanted to get away from the line of fire and started heading toward the street. He saw people look at him and run away. He saw a city bus pass him and all the passengers on the bus staring at him in horror. He wanted to make it to the bus so it could take him away from there. The bus took off. Now things became completely quiet.

He made it to the grass between the sidewalk and the street and fell there. The female officer assigned to the rear of the apartment now came running up to him. He told her, "I need an ambulance. I need an ambulance." Instead of calling for medical help, the officer started pulling at Stan's vest from under his arms in an attempt to open the Velcro straps that held it together. He tried to stop her but was too weak. He repeated, "I need help. I need an ambulance." The officer took Stan's vest off, put it on herself, and ran back to the rear of the building.

He saw another officer and called out to him. The officer didn't answer. When Stan called his name the second time a large amount of blood came out of his mouth. His lungs were filling up with blood. He lay choking on the ground. His military training kicked in at this moment, and he turned to lay on his side to put pressure on a sucking chest wound to slow his bleeding. He saw several people running from the apartment complex away from him.

He looked back toward the area of the gunfight and saw a man running toward him. He saw a paper bag and a gun in the man's hands, and knew that this was the shooter. "I just knew," Stan told me. "He's coming to get me. This is the son-of-a-bitch inside of the apartment. He's killed them all. Now he's coming to finish me off."

Stan tried to reach the snub-nosed revolver that he kept hidden in his waistband. His blood pressure had begun to fluctuate wildly. At one moment he had the energy to fight, and the next moment he would fade. Stan saw the man run up and stand over him, looking down. The man's feet were touching his body. Stan looked up at the man but couldn't see his face due to the sun's glare. He put his head down then. *Give me the f__king head shot and get it over with,* he thought. He just lay there for what seemed like an eternity. "But now I can see his face. He's looking up and down the street and then I hear it. I hear the sirens. So he runs. Great."

The chaos didn't stop then. Stan saw a police officer stop his car nearby. He held up his hand to the officer and was about to tell him that he needed an ambulance. Suddenly, several more shots rang out in the apartment. The officer turned and ran into the house. Stan was lying there, trying to fight back rage. "I was mad because I felt that I could die and nobody wanted to be with me. And now I'm going to die all alone. I remember looking at the piece of grass on the ground. That piece of grass will be here tomorrow but I might not be." He remembered just wanting to say good-bye to his wife. His son was fourteen months old at the time.

He didn't want to die. He was afraid and he was angry. Angry at what had just happened to him. Angry at the heedless actions of the officer who had knocked him aside and gone into the apartment, putting them in a very bad situation. Angry for not having enough people to do this warrant properly. He tried to take control of his fear and anger. He would stay in control and deal with it later.

Stan had never thought that he would be shot. He had worked before in one of the toughest patrol districts in the city. He had done some spectacular things. He didn't think that he was Superman, but he definitely had been "the boss." He had run things the right way—his way. There was no compromise. Now he was at the point where he really had to concentrate on staying conscious and making sure he took the next breath.

"All of a sudden," Stan told me, "I hear this applause. And I lift my head up and they're already putting the yellow crime scene tape up everywhere. And the sergeant and the guy who was shot inside originally just walked out of the apartment. And there are people now behind this crime scene tape and they're applauding these two. And I'm still lying in the dirt like a piece of shit. So then I put my head back down and I really felt awful."

The paramedics arrived shortly thereafter. They put Stan on a carry board and started to place him in the ambulance when the sergeant came running up to them. He stopped at the rear fender of the ambulance and asked one of the paramedics, "Is he going to make it?" Stan saw the paramedic make a grimace and shake his head.

The ambulance took off at high speed. On the way to the trauma hospital, Stan closed his eyes. He was a young child again, riding his tricycle in his grandmother's backyard. "And there I am sitting on the tricycle," Stan told me. "My cousin had a tricycle and I had one. I had these little plastic handlebars with the glitter. And they used to amaze me. I used to sit there for a long time just looking at the glitter. And there I was again just staring at the glitter. And that's when one of the paramedics shook me and said, 'Stan, stay with us. We haven't lost anybody yet.'" Stan thought, "You f__king liar, you probably lost the guy right before me. And I was pissed that he lied to me. But I think it worked."

The department chaplain was at the hospital when they brought Stan in. He and the priest knew each other, and he was comforted that he was not going to die alone, without someone he knew. The priest performed last rites.

Stan knew from the moment the last shot had entered his body that death was close by, but he wanted to keep fighting. He described his mindset as, "If the doctor had to cut my arms off, my legs off, whatever you had to do. I wanted to live." He had tubes shoved everywhere into his body. He listened intently to every word that was said above him. He feared that if he missed one word he would die.

His blood pressure was zeroing out. He remembers a nurse squeezing bags of blood into the vein in his leg. Much of his blood had been pumping into his lungs. He wanted to scream. He did everything he could do to live during each second that passed. It didn't matter to him what he did thirty seconds from then or the next day; he knew his life was not in vain. He had suffered these wounds trying to save somebody. He felt at peace, as if all the burdens of the world were removed from him, and felt himself letting go. He heard the doctor say then, "Okay, he's going out, let's get him upstairs."

He was surprised when he came to. *Well, I'm still alive,* he thought. Then he went out cold again. The next thing he saw was a partner with whom he had worked in a patrol beat. His partner was sitting at the foot of his bed, crying. Stan wanted to call to him and tell him not to worry, that he was all right, but he faded out again.

Several days later the breathing tube was removed from his trachea. The surgeon who had kept him alive visited him. "You were very lucky," the doctor told him. You had one cheek of your ass in God's lap. But we had a little talk and he decided to let you stay here a little bit longer." He told Stan that he had "taken everything out, like a living autopsy." His liver was split in half "like a book," and the doctor had sewn it back together. He had removed half of Stan's colon, and sewn up his diaphragm and lung. He confirmed that Stan's age and his will to live were strong contributing factors to his survival.

I asked Stan if his recovery was made more difficult because of the manner in which this incident had occurred. His injuries wouldn't have happened if it weren't for the impulsive and thoughtless acts of others. He acknowledged that a number of things about this incident were tough for him to swallow. He told me that the sergeant's position was that if there had been more personnel involved in this warrant service, more officers would have been shot.

But at the bottom line, he knew that he could not have done more than he did that day: "Even if my son or my wife were in there, I could not have done more to try to get them out. And I did everything that I could possibly do . . . so I am proud of what I did. I think that if I would have run away,

I would have had to go to the nearest police station and put my badge on the desk and say, 'You know what, I'm not worthy of this.' But I didn't run."

The sergeant was given credit for having saved Stan's life. He accepted the award he was given for his "lifesaving efforts for Stan under fire," even though the action he was credited with did not occur. The female officer who had pulled Stan's bulletproof vest off of him while he was lying on the ground wounded apologized for what she did. There was really nothing much he could say to her.

The physical wounds Stan suffered healed over time. After all, this shooting happened fifteen years ago. However, there are other unhealed psychological wounds. As I listened to him speak and sensed the nobility in him, I was reminded again of why I did this work of taking care of peace officers.

Knowing the hell he went through on his own, Stan did what one might expect "one of the good ones" to do. He started a group called the Police Survivors, made up of officers in his department who had either been shot and seriously wounded in on-duty shooting incidents or severely injured in traffic collisions. Their single mission is to support fellow officers who are similarly harmed. Sometimes just having someone near you who sincerely cares can help.

I am sure that if one were to ask the vast majority of narcotics enforcement units—and individual police officers—about the amount of emphasis they place upon officer safety and whether or not they ensure that they maintain positions of advantage when they perform, the answer would invariably be, "Of course we do!" But one of the most haunting features of listening to Stan describe the struggle he went through after being so seriously wounded was the reality that this never had to happen.

There were several red flags that were ignored because of the pressure others had succumbed to "making it happen" without the personnel, equipment, command and control, or tactical planning required to maximize the chances of safety and success. How many pounds of illegal drugs, amount of asset forfeiture money, or numbers of arrests are worth a peace officer's life?

In each of the preceding chapters, I discussed tactical pitfalls and traps that were brought about by officers' ignoring their internal discomfort that something was wrong with the picture, their uncontrolled reactions to stress exposure, and the fact that they were "captured" by their emotions or trapped into a compulsion to approach a suspicious individual without affirming first that such an approach was the right thing to do at the time. In each of these circumstances, the advantage in a tactical encounter was compromised.

Officers' advantage can also be given away when the officer expends effort to "stuff" and ignores—rather than recognizes and resolves—disturbing, irritating, or distressing events. This habitual, unconscious avoidance of unpleasant, dysphoria-producing emotional and mental conditions can actually result in officers taking a longer period of time to read a scene and the individuals involved with accuracy; and determine whether a crime has been committed, what threats exist in the incident, how imminent and serious are the threats, where their positions of advantage are, and what force options and tactics they decide to use.

This is so because the parts of the brain that perform these mental functions may have been dampened, inhibited, and impaired. What isn't continuously used starts to atrophy. The decreased functioning of the "thinking" or problem-solving parts of the brain has been conditioned and reinforced by officers' continuing efforts to avoid thinking about uncomfortable conditions rather than dominating and resolving them through acts of will.

As is well-known in law enforcement, the suspect always has a head start on the officer because they know what he or she is going to do, and the officer doesn't usually learn this until the suspect acts it out. The ability to adapt to the unexpected, rapidly changing, novel, or chaotic threat conditions without delay, hesitation, or error is a critical proficiency for officers to develop. The "how to's" of developing adaptive expertise will be discussed in a later chapter.

The loss of officer advantage can also be caused not by the individual's lack of self-control during a moment of excitation, but rather by the personal investment the victim officer had in seeing that the "red flags" connoting danger ahead be ignored so that the pursuit would not be ordered terminated.

ALL THE SIGNS WERE THERE

In 1990 in Southern California, Arturo, a veteran narcotics officer, was murdered while performing a "reverse sting." He was working in an undercover capacity, posing as a drug dealer attempting to sell cocaine to a group to which his informant had introduced him. The informant had assisted him in putting together many successful cases in which tons of illegal drugs and millions of dollars were seized.

Arturo was a proud man who was highly sensitive to criticism. Word had gotten back to him that a previous sergeant had been critical of his decision-making with a countywide narcotics suppression program Arturo had applied to. In addition, he was the lead officer in a task force consisting of thirty-six officers from a number of police agencies as well as two air support helicopters.

The "sting" was taking longer than normal to put in place because the suspects were engaged in activities that were clearly designed to detect surveillance efforts against them. No one knew that the objects of this task force, Ecuadoran drug dealers, had themselves been victims of a robbery nine months earlier in Texas. The suspects did not know that they were going to murder a police officer. Their plan was to kill the "dealer," take his stash of drugs, and resell them.

All the signs were there that the case was going to go badly. The supposed drug buyers never "flashed" or showed any money to demonstrate they had the wherewithal to purchase the drugs. They changed the location where the exchange was supposed to occur several times, and kept changing the amount of drugs they stated that they were going to buy. They went so far as to demand that the "dealer" arrive at the final meeting place by himself. They told Arturo that only he could be at the meeting place. Arturo did not stop the sting at this point. He recognized that the suspects' actions were making him uncomfortable, but he had a strong personal investment in completing the case.

The task force was organized into teams: one to provide cover for Arturo, and an arrest team responsible for taking the suspects into custody. The entire operation was to be monitored by air support. Three days prior to the deal, however, Arturo approached buddies of his from another department involved in the task force and asked them to "watch my back . . . I've got a bad feeling about this."

"Sure, man," they assured him, "we have your back." Each of the officers approached by him would have given their lives for this excellent man.

There was debate about whether or not the deal should be undertaken. Some members of the task force voiced concerns that there were too many elements of which they were not in control. Arturo's normal partner was testifying in court when he was contacted and told that the exchange was going to take place that day. He called the supervisor of their unit and demanded that the deal be shut down. The supervisor was new to the unit. He told Arturo's partner that Arturo "felt good about it" and he was not about to go against the most senior narcotics officer in the county. Arturo's partner drove to the scene as fast as his car would take him, but got there too late.

The suspects were cunning. The "buy" was to take place in a house that abutted a noise abatement wall of a busy freeway, forcing all other officers in the task force to stage on the other side of the freeway. The cover and arrest teams did not even know that shots were being fired until they heard the chilling report put out by the helicopter observer: "Shots fired. Shots fired. I have an officer down. There are multiple individuals running from the area."

The suspects had lain in wait for the "dealer" inside the front door of the house. As soon as Arturo began to walk up the driveway to the house, he was ambushed and shot with a shotgun and pistol. The courage and warrior character of this man was such that, with bullets in his heart, he shot and killed the man who had shot him.

Arturo's partner arrived on scene just in time to ride with him in the medevac helicopter to a trauma hospital. He pushed his fingers into the holes in Arturo's body in a futile attempt to stop his partner's blood from flowing out. When I first saw him after the incident, he had the blood of his partner all over him. A number of years later, he told me that he could still feel and smell Arturo's blood.

The suspects were captured, but their convictions and imprisonment did nothing to lessen the pain felt by peace officers throughout the state. In response to this incident and others in which danger signals were ignored, the California Narcotics Officers Association formed a class entitled Red Flags, which discussed how the pressure to make cases work had led involved officers to ignore danger signals prior to shots being fired.

I have listened to scores of peace officers as they affirm that they would "never allow such incidents to occur" in their departments. For example, one said, "We would never permit the undercover officer to be responsible for decision-making and planning about the case as well, and we would never run an operation with the red flags visible in this tragedy." When I show videos of peace officers being murdered because they did not act decisively and forcefully enough in the face of assault, I am told that "we would never allow such circumstances to exist in our department."

Officer expectations are also based upon the appearance, dress, and behavior of the individuals with whom they come into contact. The term *profiling* creates a great deal of sensitivity when it is mentioned. The reality is, however, that we use expectations and judgments about people all the time, normally without being aware that we are doing so. When we observe someone's appearance, there is a strong tendency to associate that person with the characteristics of those similar to that person we have seen or heard about in the past—and come to an assumption or expectation of how they are likely to act.

I have spoken with officers who were shot and wounded at a domestic disturbance call by a woman dressed in a bikini who had hidden a small pistol in the back of her suit bottom. Who would expect a young woman in a swimsuit to be a threat? A number of times, elderly people startled officers when they pulled out firearms and shot them.

The ability to prevent a lethal assault against a peace officer is a highly perishable proficiency. A number of component parts of the individual—some of which are attitudinal, some mental, some emotional, and some physical—must be maintained at peak or near-peak levels of performance. They must be practiced and improved upon, and officers can never allow themselves to be satisfied that they have done enough to ensure that they return home to their loved ones.

5

CONDITIONING VICTORIOUS HABITS

PEAK PERFORMANCE AND VICTORY

The ability to be victorious in one's life and work is not something that peace officers can take for granted. Peak performance is accomplished through the continuing commitment to oneself to achieve never-ending progress and the quest for excellence in mental, emotional, behavioral, and personal fitness levels.

Even those who are not instinctively warriors can condition themselves to perform as warriors—through the formation of habits that natural warriors perform when under duress. In this process, the individual works to overcome difficult, distressing, or disturbing obstacles without permitting a lessening of effort or feelings to occur that could give him or her the idea that "this is too much for me—I wasn't ready for this—I'm not sure I'm prepared to handle this."

Conversely, it is just as possible to degrade officers' ability to display peak performance through the damaging influence of compromise, complacency, or doing their work and living their lives at just mediocre levels of effort or commitment to excellence. Conditioning for peak performance only occurs when individuals perform purposeful acts of will that require them to stretch themselves to achieve levels of fitness or skill of which they were not previously capable.

Whether they participate in physical fitness training or not, most people are at least familiar with the concept of physical conditioning. Mental fitness, emotional fitness, and mastery fitness, however, are not as well understood. Yet the *integration* of physical, mental, emotional, and mastery conditioning exerts the greatest possible influence upon officers' success or failure, personal health, and the quality of life they enjoy.

Peace officers do spend a substantial amount of time practicing procedural skills during the early parts of their career. After a short number of months or years, however, the successes they have achieved in their work sometimes bring them feelings of confidence that their ability and experience alone can be depended upon for victory without much in the way of further practice; for example, "I don't need to practice, I am an expert in this task."

ADAPTATION TO CHANGING CONDITIONS

Yes, the skills, techniques, and habits developed by veteran officers worked for them in the past. But are their habits and the ways that they are predisposed to approach their work going to work for *this case* at *this time*—with conditions they may never have seen before?

Without continuing skills practice in responding to a range of *unexpected* and *startling* conditions—and learning how to maintain intentional thought and purposeful action in response to these conditions—officers cannot be certain that what worked for them before will work on this night when they are surprised by the sudden introduction of an unexpected threat.

The performance of the same action over time makes that action familiar to the individual doing it, and comes to appear as normalcy in the individual's brain. Officers can then become predisposed to depend upon those now-familiar actions—regardless of the level of success they may have doing so (Lehner, Seyed-Solorforough, O'Connor, Sak, & Mullin, 1997). Rigid or habitual actions in response to unexpected threat are likely—at least in part—responsible for officers continuing to use tactics they had begun even after those tactics have ceased to be effective (Staw, Sandelands, & Dutton, 1981).

UNEXPECTED EVENTS

It is hard to imagine anyone being able to overpower Rick physically. He is an imposing figure, standing well over six feet tall, and weighs more than 250 pounds. Even now in his retirement, he continues to be a strong physical presence. One constant in his police career was the confidence he and other officers had in his tactical skills and physical strength.

Rick and his partner were assigned to a plainclothes tactical assignment. In a tactical squad, officers were free from responding to calls for service in a specified area to seek out perpetrators of crime as well as go to the "hot calls."

Members of a family that lived in the subsidized public housing projects called the police department and complained that their grandfather was threatening them with a gun. They lived on the seventh floor. Two uniformed officers joined Rick and his partner, who were the first to arrive.

They knocked on the door of the apartment listed in the complaint call. No one answered the door the first time they knocked. The second time they knocked on the door, a sheet of paper was slipped from underneath the apartment's front door. It was some type of advertisement for armed security guards. Rick's immediate impression was that the person inside the apartment was telling them that he was armed.

There was an apartment directly across the hallway. Rick and his partner knocked on the door and told the occupants to withdraw to the farthest reaches of their apartment. The officers used the neighbors' front door and a hall closet in their entryway for cover, "in case the guy opened the door shooting."

"So anyway," Rick told me, "we're talking and knocking on the door—he was a sixty-one-year-old black man. He was on medication for some mental problems. We kept talking to him. You know, 'John, open the door. Come on, it's no big deal.'"

The front door opened very slowly. Inside the door was a six- or seven-foot hallway that led into a living room. The sixty-one-year-old man had backed up and was standing silent and motionless at the end of the hallway, facing the officers. Rick and his partner entered the apartment then, along with the two uniformed officers. One of the uniforms started looking around for a gun or other weapon. The other uniform remained outside and was getting information from the family members.

Rick was the lead officer in the hallway facing the disturbed man. He held his gun in a low-ready position. As he usually did, he wore a shoulder holster over a T-shirt but underneath a pullover "hoodie" sweatshirt. "I could see both of his hands. They were empty. But I'd had other experiences where a guy in the same situation had hid the gun under the pillow on a couch or put it somewhere and all of a sudden his hands are clean but you're talking to him and now he dives and now we're wrestling and he's got his gun. So rather than pull my sweatshirt up, put my gun back in my holster, and snap it, I just tucked it in my pants, figuring, if I need it, instead of going 'uh-oh,' all I have to do is take it and go 'boom boom.'"

Rick recalled that he was "schmoozing" the silent man. He said to him, "Let us take a look around. I'm sure we're not going to find anything. We'll be on our way. It's no problem. You know, we'll be out of your hair in five minutes and we're done with you."

Rick took out his handcuffs and told the man, "Look, just so that everything's okay and nobody gets hurt, let me put the cuffs on you and I'm sure we're not going to find anything, and when we're done, I'll take the cuffs off and we'll leave and that's the end of it."

When he reached forward and took hold of the man's right hand to put the handcuffs on him, the man abruptly pulled away. Rick attempted to calm him, and said, "Come on, man, just relax. Let's just get this over with and we'll be on our way."

He again attempted to take control of the man's right hand, and again the man pulled away. The third time, Rick was able to get one cuff on when the man pulled away again. Throughout this time, the man had not uttered a sound. Now one handcuff was swinging freely. They began to struggle. Their efforts caused them to move into the living room. The man's back was to a couch against the wall, and Rick was facing him and the couch in the middle of the living room. The man maintained his silence.

"We're struggling," Rick recalled. "I'm trying to get hold of his other arm. I never even felt it happen, but he took my gun out of my belt.

We're locked. We're close. And this guy might have been, I'm going to say, maybe five-foot nine, and maybe one hundred eighty or one hundred ninety pounds. Short and stocky. . . . So as we're struggling, all of a sudden I hear 'pop.' I start looking around and I'm thinking to myself, 'who the f__k is shooting?'"

Rick felt a burn then, and looked down to see that his shirt was on fire. He yelled to his partner, "He's got my gun!" Rick turned to the suspect and saw him coming to shoot him again. His partner had also heard the "pop" and fired three times at the suspect. Another officer then jumped on the suspect and, with his two hands over the suspect's hands holding the gun, turned the muzzle of Rick's gun until it faced the suspect's body. Rick heard four more gunshots. The gunfire stopped after that.

Still standing, Rick leaned against the wall. He knew with his entire being that he must stay awake. "'Cause I know it's bad. You know, like the old John Wayne thing—'He was gut shot.'"

At the time this incident occurred, there was only one portable radio in each police car. Rick's partner did not have a radio, and Rick's radio had somehow gotten underneath the man's body during their struggle. The officer outside the apartment had begun screaming when gunshots were heard, and was not making coherent statements to dispatch personnel.

Rick's partner took the radio from the hand of the screaming officer and notified dispatch that "we've got a police officer shot up here!" His partner walked him out of the apartment and down the hallway to the seventh-floor elevator. Officers working in the projects knew that they would receive medical aid much more quickly if they waited outside of the building for the ambulance to come.

His partner asked him if he wanted to be driven in the squad car. Rick doesn't know why he thought this way, but he remembers thinking that he must not sit down. He thought that if he did that, he would die for sure. He couldn't lie down in the car because they wouldn't be able to close the door, either his feet or head would stick out. A police vehicle normally used for transporting several people at one time was used to take him to the university hospital. They took him with one officer holding his head and another holding him by his feet. Rick's thoughts when he got to the hospital ranged from imagining he was dying to telling himself he had to actively try to take control of what was happening to him.

The bullet had entered the lower front area of Rick's body in a downward path. It took off part of his kidney and severed his colon. It missed his spine by one-half of an inch. The doctors were worried about the risk of peritonitis due to the fact that his colon had been severed. They put packing inside of him. Three times a day nurses would take out the packing, clean him, and put new saline-soaked packing inside. The pain he experienced was brutal. He dealt with the pain and struggled to get through the early parts of his recovery. This went on for twelve weeks. During this time his body was held together with leather straps, so to speak. He could not eat or drink on his own for a month.

It is difficult for most peace police officers to understand the struggles the wounded officer is going to go through to recover from being shot, stabbed, or bludgeoned. After the initial impact of the incident lessens, visitors leave their bedside. The officer and their immediate family must control the damage that has been done to their body and soul on their own. While the hospital room is filled with well wishers, the wounded officer will not disclose the pain and fear they are going through.

Above all else, the officer feels that he or she must put on a happy face and laugh with his or her buddies about what happened. Such officers experience a great deal of social pressure to avoid appearing weak or vulnerable. They follow the script written for law-enforcement officers since the earliest days of crime fighting: "Keep your feelings to yourself. Don't admit that when you are alone, you have doubts and fears. Keep it light and act cool."

The nurse who entered Rick's hospital room was referred to as the "bag lady." She was the one who showed patients how to use the colostomy bag that the surgeons had attached to his side. He did not want to learn how to use the apparatus. "I was in denial—I didn't want to eat when I could eat because I didn't want to have to worry about it. And then little by little, I could manage it—and I had to make sure I didn't eat after five because if you're in bed at night and you have to go, you just go. And if you're in the wrong position, the force of the stool will sometimes break the seal away and you wake up and here you are at thirty-four years old and you shit all over yourself." The colostomy bag was removed after six weeks.

Rick wasn't angry with himself, but he knew what had caused him to be shot. "And that was not to secure my weapon better. But I did what I did through the experience of needing to get to it quick."

I asked him if he had practiced quick draws where he wore his firearm in plain clothes. "No," he answered; "it's something you wouldn't do in soft clothes. That's something that I don't think anybody would do and I never practiced really quick draw in uniform. I always felt that I could kind of size up a situation and know when I needed my weapon to be out. But because of prior experience I thought I was doing the right thing. My experience and what I thought I was doing right—for this particular situation, it was wrong."

Few peace officers spend a great deal of time and effort practicing fast draws where they keep their firearm when they are in a plainclothes assignment, or where they carry their firearm when they are off duty. Even when their firearms training consists of more than just qualifying tests, there is usually not an emphasis upon including unexpected and unplanned uses of lethal force.

Officers who take part in scenario training and are wearing the mandatory face masks already expect that they are going to get involved in a shooting—and there is, therefore, little in the way of practice provided to them in responding to lethal threat events that shock, startle, or disorient them.

Rick described himself as a person who needed a goal to work as hard as he was capable. He found one in the yearly triathlon held in his city. He started serious training on April 1, a short number of months since he'd been shot. The news media discovered that he was attempting to achieve this difficult goal. When he completed the full triathlon, his achievement was broadcast in a manner that made him feel even better. As Rick laughingly put it, "It was my fifteen minutes of fame."

He knew then that if he could do a triathlon, he had overcome the last major hurdle he had faced in his recovery: "If I could do this, I was ready. Physically, mentally, I was ready to go back to work. So like three weeks later, I went back—right back to what I was doing [before the shooting]—my same partner. And we stayed together another eight years."

HOW GOOD IS GOOD ENOUGH?

I learned a simple truth over the course of thirty years responding to the traumas and tragedies that occur in law enforcement. The officers who survived serious wounds and injuries—who were victorious in body, mind, and soul—had prepared for these experiences well before they were hurt.

"Just okay" levels of fitness, achievement, and skill in how they lived and worked were not good enough for these individuals. They possessed *and fueled* an internal drive to achieve and perform beyond the norm. They did not experience a defeated feeling from obstacles they faced in work, sports, or living. Instead, the obstacles provided additional motivation for them to *stretch their ability and strength* to overcome and vanquish them.

In the early days of training with the use of paint-filled munitions, I observed a number of officers stop fighting and cease their efforts as soon as the Simunition bullet struck them—even when they were struck in a non-vital area like the hand, arm, or leg. When a training officer asked them why they had stopped, they replied, "Because I've been shot." Their expectation was that, if they were shot, the fight was over for them.

The police officers that contributed their experiences to this book had a common trait: while there were moments where they thought that they were going to die, they persevered. This is a topic only sometimes discussed in law enforcement. In describing military actions, however, an excellent book, *Lone Survivor: The Eyewitness Account of Operation Redwing and the Lost Heroes of SEAL Team 10* (Luttrell, Marcusi, and Robinson, 2007) provides a dramatic, detailed picture of what it takes to persevere against seemingly overwhelming odds.

Ensuring that the will to live takes primacy when a peace officer is wounded requires a foundation of determination that must be built into the individual's daily life and conditioned over several years at the highest levels of performance of which one is capable. Overcoming the obstacles of fatigue, distress, difficulty, or discomfort through purposeful acts of will develops the confidence, competence, and stamina that officers will need if they are seriously assaulted. To fight successfully and victoriously for one's life is a trait not to be taken for granted.

AVOIDING THE TENDENCY TO GIVE IN OR GIVE UP

The term *anhedonia* (anti-hedonism or anti-pleasure seeking) refers to a weakening in, and inability to, take pleasure from normally enjoyed things, people, or events. It very often shows itself as a withdrawal from strengthening activity.

Anhedonic withdrawal is often created in the aftermath of events in which individuals experience feelings of helplessness or loss. It is, in fact, a primary symptom seen in peace officers who get depressed, and is secondary to posttraumatic stress reactions. The experience of anhedonia can be likened to wearing eyeglasses covered with human waste—everything the person sees looks crappy to him or her.

Two of the most commonly occurring features of anhedonic feelings are the loss of vigor and drive in the person, and a loss of motivation to engage in activities that previously brought pleasure or added to their strength. The commitment to strengthening themselves, for example, with physical exercise is replaced by an "Ah, I don't feel like it" rationalization. People are, by consequence, weakened by these self-defeating behaviors.

Victorious habits will be built upon an officer's total commitment to achieve peak performance in whatever they do, no matter what mood or circumstance they may find themselves in. "Just okay" should never be good enough for the life they live on this earth. In an emergency situation, the brain will not do what an officer hopes it will do. It will do what that officer has trained and conditioned it to do over time through hundreds of repetitions.

The performance of skills in self-defense and uses of force to control a resistant or assaultive subject, for example, can be performed at relatively proficient levels by most peace officers who successfully go through the

Academy and Field Training activities. The same skills, however, are highly likely to be altered—and impaired—when the officer becomes fatigued.

For example, Commander Jeffrey Johnson of the Long Beach, California, Police Department writes about a threshold of fatigue that peace officers may experience. He defines the fatigue threshold as "The sudden physical exhaustion experienced during a force encounter when an officer cannot effectively perform to either control a suspect or defend himself (Johnson, 2010).

Although most of the discussion that occurs regarding peace officer fatigue will focus upon physical behaviors, law enforcement leaders and trainers should also be aware that officers are affected by fatigue of a mental, emotional, and spiritual nature as well. The term "spiritual" does not refer to religious feeling here but, rather, the drive to perform one's work and life activities as part of a never-ending quest for mastery--that is, to maximize and fulfill one's highest possible potential as a human being, peace officer, athlete, spouse, parent, friend, et cetera.

MENTAL FATIGUE

Mental fatigue is not experienced in the same way as physical fatigue (i.e., feeling tired; or a lessening of strength, energy, and stamina). Rather, mental fatigue shows itself as lapses or decreases in the level and accuracy in officer vigilance, and a reduction in the amount of objects they scrutinize in the environment.

It does not take too many times of responding to silent alarms, 9-1-1 hang-up calls, family disturbances, or walking up to a vehicle they have stopped for officers' brains to become habituated to what they have experienced on a daily basis. Events that are now familiar provide feelings of normalcy for the officer—things appear to be as they should be.

Continuing vigilance and attention to "what doesn't belong here?" at a scene can create tension or irritation over time and threaten to wear down the mental stamina required for intense concentration while under duress. At this point, the brain is attempting to "relax" or "take a mental break."

Attempts to become more comfortable dampen and dull the intensity of focus of attention and concentration officers can bring to bear upon conditions to which they are exposed. A number of officers I assisted after a critical event acknowledged that, "All the danger signs were there. I saw them. But I didn't pay attention to them."

EMOTIONAL FATIGUE

One of the saddest interactions I had following an officer-involved shooting occurred a number of years ago. An expert and highly respected police officer assigned to his department's SWAT team had been murdered during a dynamic entry into a barricaded suspect's residence.

The team leader told me that, prior to the entry, he felt a strong concern that they were walking into trouble they might not be able to get out of: "I was ... filled with a feeling of dread," he said. But like most elite tactical officers, the members of the team stated that, "Hey, we're the best—we're not going to let anything like nervous feelings like that stop us. We're the ones who take care of business when others can't."

Emotional fatigue most often occurs over time as a consequence of the practice of "stuffing" one's conscious attention to distressing emotions or feelings of helplessness that arise. Peace officers have to develop a callous attitude or insulation over personal feelings that protects them from emotional harm or injury encountered in the course of their duties. Problems arise when they apply that attempt at numbing to all aspects of their lives.

Blocking out one's awareness of distressed emotions works while the officer is performing work tasks, but law enforcement's tradition and practice of "stuffing" emotions rather than mastering them through purposeful acts of will has denied many officers the opportunity to achieve success coping effectively with the issues of their lives. When emotions are ignored, officers are also engaging in the avoidance of problem-solving activities that could resolve the pain they were feeling. Examples include tragic events like child deaths or fallen officers.

I do not agree with the simple dismissal of powerful emotions; for example, feeling like, "If I don't think about it, and no one sees it, then I don't have a problem." Even if officers are unconcerned with their personal emotional health, the emotional fatigue that develops from the "excess baggage" that many officers carry *impairs their ability to recognize danger signals*—the critical intuitive reactions that are telling them, "Something is wrong with this picture." It also prevents them from taking advantage of whatever good things and happiness are available to them in their lives.

The ugly feelings that officers expend so much energy to remove from their conscious mind do not go away. They just affect officers in unconscious and uncontrolled ways, and are expressed indirectly (such as the short-fused, angry discharge officers sometimes take out on family members or irritating subjects/citizens) without self-control.

Conscious recognition that one has experienced a jolt of unpleasant emotion permits officers to countermand the harmful consequences of ugly events. Conditioning themselves to confront and resolve distressed emotions directly and proactively will assist officers in recognizing the real source of the emotion (rather than displacing or projecting the distress onto people and things that had nothing to do with them). Doing so allows them the license to feel their feelings without negative self-judgment, and then put that behind them by moving forward with intent and purpose. Stuffing, ignoring, or denying an emotional event just makes work fitness more difficult to maintain.

MASTERY CONDITIONING

Mastery conditioning predisposes individuals to function at or near peak levels of performance when confronted with unexpected or difficult obstacles. The formation of mastery habits are developed by the individual continuously "stretching" him- or herself and his or her ability to achieve ever greater levels of proficiency, skill, and success in work, life, and interpersonal tasks. Nothing should be done at "just okay" or complacent levels of effort.

At the end of the game in which the underdog Houston Rockets won the 1994–1995 NBA championship, Coach Rudy Tomjanovich was asked to comment upon the fact that few had predicted their victory. His comment was profound, and spoke to an important element underlying the quest for mastery: "Never underestimate the heart of a champion."

I believe that most peace officers take the treasures they are given in life for granted. For example, they don't spend a great deal of time being conscious of and celebrating that their family is safe today. They work in a profession that brings them honor. They (hopefully) haven't lost their home. And the things that bother them and occupy their mind are transient. It is a truism that, in law enforcement as well as in most walks of life, "Tough times don't last. Tough people do."

It is for this reason that I have always been greatly concerned with the number of peace officers who engage in self-defeating or self-destructive behaviors that ruin their chances for a successful life. Working in a law enforcement agency sometimes means that, for the rest of their adult careers, many will be negatively affected by a sometimes-dysfunctional organizational culture and character. The problematic features of law enforcement organizations can and often do distress police officers more than the street or institution does.

When officers' minds are preoccupied with things that frustrate and distress them, they are expending less effort focusing upon and driving themselves toward the goals that bring them feelings of victory, achievement, and empowerment. But if those officers persist, they can counteract the harmful effects of troubling work conditions through self-directed acts of will.

Performing productive, self-empowering behaviors that bring feelings of accomplishment to the individual has an impact upon the brain that is similar to antidepressant medication. It dampens and inhibits the worry, sadness, and feelings of futility that often accompany dysphoric moods. Acting so on a continual basis actually changes the brain's structure and functions, increasing nerve connections and directing new nerve pathways to perform the strengthening or achievement behavior as a now-automatic response.

Driving oneself toward mastery in all areas of performance and living has a curative effect upon an individual. Almost all the problems and difficulties that are injurious to officers contain elements of feeling the loss of control or helplessness. The act of empowerment counters what could otherwise turn into some form of a psychology of defeat. A continuing drive toward excellence both as a cop and as a spouse, parent, friend, or athlete ensures that officers prevent any self-appraisal along the lines of "this is too much for me" when faced with unfamiliar, unexpected, or uncontrolled tasks.

"I NEVER THOUGHT IT WOULD HAPPEN TO ME"

On the night he fought for his life, Mack was a young officer with five years of law enforcement experience. He was "living large and feeling good" at this period of his life and career. He was excited about his recent selection to the department's Special Enforcement Unit and was working as a field training officer until his transfer took place.

He was working the graveyard shift. His trainee had called in sick. He was free to hunt criminals and take people to jail, and would get off on time without having to concern himself with a trainee. It was going to be a good night.

He was patrolling an area where a high number of burglaries had occurred recently. Just after midnight, and about halfway down the block, he saw a figure riding a bicycle in his direction. The bicycle had no lights on it. There was enough ambient light for the officer to see a male figure dressed in black or another dark color. His bicycle was weaving back and forth over part of the street.

An adult male riding a bicycle after midnight in a residential area hit by burglaries? Mack felt immediately that this was someone to stop and investigate. As he got closer to the male and slowed his vehicle, he saw that the male was big. Mack later found out that his assailant was six-foot three and weighed 270 pounds.

As soon as he observed the police vehicle, the bicyclist made an abrupt left turn onto the sidewalk. Mack followed him and put out on the radio that he was intending to stop a suspicious person. He was driving slowly, parallel to the bicycle and going in the same direction. The bicyclist stopped immediately when Mack illuminated him with his light.

Mack left his vehicle, holding his flashlight, as the rider got off the bicycle and put down the kickstand. The suspicious male was very calm as Mack approached him.

Mack had been involved in physical fights before this, but they had happened when he was attempting to put someone in custody. He was confident about his physical strength and ability. He hadn't paid much attention to improving himself through training efforts, because with five years of success, he, like many other officers, thought that he "knew it all." He did only what was required of him.

When he imagined himself getting involved in an on-duty shooting incident, he always had time to prepare. He believed that he would handle himself well if and when it happened. However, he could not have been more wrong.

He calmly called to the man, "What's up?"

The man answered back, "What's up, Officer?" He turned so that his eyes were locked on Mack's eyes.

Mack later told me that this action should have set off alarm bells, "But it didn't. I thought, 'That's strange, why is he doing that?'" In the next moment, the man brandished a fifteen-inch-long screwdriver whose end had been ground to a sharp point. He charged at Mack with the screwdriver extended in his left hand.

"It took me a second to process what was happening, and even then I didn't believe it," Mack admitted. "A full second, and I stood and did nothing—shocked."

He told me that as soon as the attack against him registered, his instinct for survival came to the forefront. He was not engaging in planned or decided-upon tactics or performing procedures he had learned in training. "There was nothing to hide behind," he told me. "I started backing up as fast as I could, almost at a run. I drew my handgun and started firing it blindly as soon as it was out of my holster. My first two rounds were in the street right in front of me, and then [the suspect] was on me, yelling and swinging the weapon at me. I could feel the swinging motion of his arm as he attempted to stab me. I kept firing point blank into him, but he was not stopping. I remember thinking, 'I'm missing! I can't believe I'm missing!'

"We moved backward, me trying to push him off with my left hand while firing with my right, and him holding on to my uniform jacket with his right, trying to stab me with his left." Mack tripped and fell to the ground on his back. "He dove on top of me while I continued to fire at him one-handed. I put my left foot up in an effort to keep him off of me but that did not work. He was now on top of me, still trying to stab me. I kept shooting. He was still not stopping. The only conscious thought I had during this incident was, 'Go for the head shot.' I brought up my handgun and tried to shoot him in the head. He was still trying to get the shank in me, and was pushing down on me with his free hand and body weight. I finally saw an opening, pulled him down closer to me, put the muzzle of my handgun on top of his head and pulled the trigger."

The suspect went limp on top of Mack. "A hot jet of blood, brain, and skull debris then erupted from his head wound and into my face. It was like a hose. It went into my mouth, and I immediately thought of what it tastes like when you have a bloody nose. I pushed him off of me and stood up. Dogs were barking. I reached for my radio and it was not there. I was shaking violently. I wiped off my face with my left forearm the best that I could."

Mack felt overwhelmed by what had just happened to him. "I was not prepared, and continued to shake uncontrollably. Other officers arrived to assist. One of them had to physically take my weapon from me and place it into my holster because I could not do it myself. I kept staring at [the suspect] and at the blood. I could not believe what had just happened. I was covered in blood. My weapon, my leather gear, my uniform was soaked from the waist up. I had a large hole in my uniform jacket, through my right sleeve, and into the front of the jacket between the jacket and my uniform."

The incident changed Mack. He no longer looked upon an officer-involved shooting as a much-imagined entry ticket into the "fraternity" of officers who had undergone such an experience. He took training and practice much more seriously thereafter. He sought out opportunities to learn and to better his tactical skills. He began to read articles and books about training and performance in law enforcement. He changed his lifestyle habits because he now understood how easily a cop can die if he or she is ill prepared for an encountered threat.

When his assailant had turned away from him as Mack walked up, he was slow to adapt to the change because he *expected* or envisioned how he would investigate what this man was doing and, hopefully, find him guilty of something that would result in an arrest. It had always gone that way, after all. When the actions of the suspect were different than what he *expected*, it took time to reorient himself.

Over the course of my career, I have heard hundreds of officers describe their reactions when they encountered a threat they had never experienced before, one that they did not expect and for which they were not mentally prepared. Their typical response would be, "This is not supposed to happen. This guy was doing things different from the way I expected."

HOW THE IMPORTANT LESSONS ARE LEARNED

I haven't met too many people in law enforcement who learn the important lessons—the ones that will keep them alive and well—until they go through some type of event that bursts the bubble of denial that "it's not going to happen to me." Whether having to fight for their life with someone who is trying not to escape but to kill them, or witnessing incidents in which other officers are killed, surviving near-death incidents changes police officers, with regard to their attitudes, training efforts, and uses of judgment.

Law enforcement work came fairly easily to Ray. He had been an active, aggressive young man who drove himself to sometimes-extreme achievements. Prior to becoming a police officer, for example, Ray had competed internationally in blue-water fishing tournaments, a sport where fish are hunted with spear guns deep beneath the surface of the ocean without the use of any oxygen or diving aids other than swim fins.

Ray grew up in a law enforcement family in a suburban beach community. His father was a legendary police officer in Southern California. From the time he was a young child, Ray had listened to the stories his father and his police buddies exchanged about the dangerous and exciting incidents in which they had been victorious. By the time he became a police cadet at age eighteen, he fully expected that when he became a police officer he would be "the same as the guys who ran at 110 miles per hour—hard chargers who were having a good time doing the job."

Ray generated a good deal of arrests and developed a reputation as a "squared-away cop." He was a proactive, aggressive officer who never thought much about the possible consequences of his actions, including jumping off buildings to chase people or getting into dangerous foot pursuits by himself, once "for a broken light on a car." His number-one concern was to catch the suspect, no matter the cost: "I felt good doing the things I was doing. But I shouldn't have been doing it."

There was never a moment in the earliest part of his career where he felt vulnerable or fearful. He had ultimate confidence in his ability to overcome whatever obstacle or threat came his way. He had good verbal ability, was in good physical condition, and stayed in control when confronted with emotionally upset, resistive, or assaultive people.

After about five years in patrol, he began to work as an undercover, plainclothes detective on the department's narcotics enforcement unit. Given the small size of the police agency, his unit was also responsible for gang enforcement and fugitive apprehension. His hair had grown long and he maintained a scruffy, bandit-like appearance with a drooping moustache and two-pointed goatee.

Ray had recently been visiting his father and showed him his new "quick draw" holster. His father's response was to tell him, "That's not a retention holster. Get rid of it." "No, Dad," Ray responded, "it's fast. I can wear it in my belt and get to my gun quick."

On the day that changed his life, Ray and two other investigators were assisting uniformed officers by taking a parole violator into custody. His partners approached the suspect's house from the front. Ray was in an alleyway at the rear of the house. It didn't appear to be a big deal. "As soon as the cops go in the front," Ray told me, "the guy comes running out [the back] and starts to run across backyards."

As noted earlier, undercover officers cannot always follow, and often violate, the majority of officer safety practices. When working undercover, for example, officers cannot be seen carrying radios. They do not carry most or all of the equipment that is used to protect and assist uniformed officers in dealing with dangerous people.

"My boss did not have a radio either. I watched the guy jump four walls. It looked like he was going to go around to the front of the neighboring houses. I called to him, and he turns and sees a guy who has long hair and a beard. I'm yelling at him not to move."

Ray showed his badge, and the wanted parolee turned and ran. The chase was on. In Ray's mind, you didn't run from him. No matter what it took, he would run you down and take you into custody. He began to chase the man over fences and through backyards. The fleeing man began to fatigue. When he realized that he would not be able to get over a wall that was in front of him, he turned and looked behind him. His only way out was through Ray.

Ray was surprised by the man's actions. Suspects had always run before, and he had always been the one chasing them until he caught them and placed them under arrest. Ray knew at this moment that this one was different. He was not going to try to escape. He was going to attempt to hurt or kill Ray to get away.

With his head and shoulders down, the man charged at Ray. Ray punched him several times around the head, but his assailant outweighed him by twenty to thirty pounds. The punches were not having a great effect. They shoved each other around for several seconds, and then Ray heard the "clank" sound of metal on concrete.

He looked down and saw his gun on the ground between them. He thought, "Hey, that looks just like my gun." He saw his attacker's right hand go for the gun. Ray tried to pull him back. He saw the man's hand touch the gun, and then everything went dark. The last thought he was conscious of was his realization that he was fighting for his life: if he did not stop this individual, he would be killed.

When Ray's partners ran up to the two of them, they had no idea what he had just gone through. It was evident that Ray had overcome the attack against him and was able to save his life, but he had no idea how it happened. He had to admit to himself how close he had been to being killed.

"I was in a haze for a week. I had nightmares that my gun fell while I was fighting with a crook. He's reaching for it. I try to stop him, but can't seem to move fast enough. When he's about to shoot me, I wake up." He'd been in scuffles before but had always had the upper hand. He saw now that all of the times he had conveniently expected that "this life-threatening stuff happens to other officers but it's not going to happen to me" were foolish. It was no longer a question of *if* such an event would happen, but *when*.

Ray had been in good physical condition prior to this incident. Because he had never really been tested, he *expected*, as many peace officers do, that his "pretty good" levels of strength and stamina would be enough. Now he understood that true officer safety requires maximum effort on the part of the officer him- or herself.

His response to the fear and vulnerability he had felt is, in fact, what provides the foundation for victory when officers are fighting for their life. After this incident Ray's daily activity consisted of a total rededication to maximum-effort strength and work fitness conditioning. His effort was fueled by the memory of his uncertainty and the real possibility of defeat when his punches had no effect upon the suspect's attempts to overpower him.

The image of that moment came to him whenever he was fatigued or complacent in his practice, and created a renewed surge of effort. He changed his diet completely, forgoing the fifteen-cent burritos and other fast foods he used to eat, and began consuming only fresh, whole, raw, nutrient-dense foods. He also lessened the number of beers he imbibed when he went out with his buddies.

Ray took stock of the equipment he carried. He changed how he carried his firearm and ensured his use of a radio in every field activity. He began to rehearse quick draws in plainclothes and off duty, and greatly increased his efforts in weaponless defense techniques.

However, victory by an officer over an individual who is in the act of attempting to murder him or her will not be achieved by physical fitness alone. It is within the mind and the amount and quality of practice in mental conditioning—that is, the officer's use of judgment, decision-making, and self-regulation under conditions of duress—that the chances for overcoming lethal threat are enhanced.

Ray knew he had been lucky in the past. He now expended a great deal of time and effort visualizing and preparing for as many difficult and dangerous situations as possible. He conditioned his thinking and decision-making to be much more concerned with consequence than he had been in the past.

He had heard about officers who were killed or wounded in a gunfight because they did not possess the necessary armament or equipment. Because his department was small in number and equipment (i.e., one patrol vehicle on most work shifts), officers did "pretty much everything on our own."

In anticipation of "the big one," he put together a duffel bag filled with many boxes of bullets and several magazines for both his firearm and rifle, and carried them everywhere with him in the trunk of his car. He continued the mental practice of using visualizations of a range of different circumstances he could potentially encounter, and planned how he would engage each different condition. His commitment to preparing himself for the unexpected threat was tested some months later.

Ray was headed toward the department firing range for his monthly qualifying requirement on February 26, 2010, when he heard garbled radio traffic from the department dispatcher. The transmission reported that the county sheriffs had put out an "1199" call, the most urgent code in that area for police officers. It meant that shots had been fired, and that officers were down and needed immediate, urgent help.

Two sheriff deputies and an agent from the Department of Forestry and Fire Protection had tried to serve a search warrant that morning at 9:40 on a man living in a mobile home in a rural area. As they approached the residence, one of the deputies, a homicide detective, had been shot in the head with a bullet fired from an assault rifle and died immediately. The barricaded suspect had fortified himself with a number of assault rifles and hundreds of bullets for this moment. The other two officers ran for cover and started exchanging gunfire with the man in the house.

Ray switched to the county sheriff's radio frequency to get a better idea of what was happening. "It was scary to hear the fear in deputies' voices. You've heard excited voices asking for backup. This was different. They were pleading for help."

He decided to stay off the radio regarding his location and intended to go to the scene to back up the other officers. He was thoughtful about not disrupting cops who were taking fire and asking for help, but unable to communicate because their transmissions were being "covered up" by other officers responding to their aid. "It was pandemonium. There were several voices on the radio screaming. There was chaos. The gun battle was still in progress. They needed help from SWAT."

Ray decided to go to the scene and give whatever help was needed. He was about two minutes away. Because of the armament used by the suspect, his plan was to use his AR-15. He felt himself getting "amped up." Not wanting to get out of control, he took a slow, deep breath, held it for a second, and then with his first breath out, because he was more in control, realized that his rifle wasn't loaded. He felt himself calm down, and spent the two minutes preparing himself, his mind-set, and his physical readiness to take action.

Over thirty police vehicles were blocking the approach to the scene of the gun battle, forcing responding officers to run a distance through the maze of cars while under fire from the house. Ray grabbed the rifle and his duffle bag and made his way through the cars to reach his partner. When he got there, his partner and several other officers yelled that they were out of ammunition. All of them grabbed several magazines and bullets from Ray's duffle.

The dead deputy was dragged past Ray. He didn't look. He was focused on shooting into the mobile home. He heard bullets whizzing past his head. The suspect was walking around in the trailer, firing .30-30 shells out of the front and rear windows at the cops.

Ray went through several rifle magazines and, like all the other cops there, fired blindly into the windows of the trailer. The gun battle raged for an hour and a half. It was later determined that the cops had fired over fifteen hundred rounds, while the suspect shot three hundred. SWAT teams arrived and took command of the scene.

Ray and the other officers were told to stand down and withdraw. It was hard giving up the fight to SWAT. He turned to his partner and said, "Let's head back, he killed one of theirs. Let them take over." They couldn't withdraw at first because there were now about one hundred cops on scene. With some effort, Ray and his partner made it to the rear of a neighboring building.

Word spread that a police officer from Ray's department had been shot. He was one of Ray's best friends there. Hearing that the wounded officer had been rushed to the hospital, Ray and his partner got into the back of a Highway Patrol vehicle to give their support to their fallen comrade.

The patrol vehicle was traveling at 115 miles per hour when Ray got the news (via radio) that the officer was dead. Ray had been screaming at the driver to drive slower and now told him, "Hey, asshole, he's f__king dead, you can slow down."

Ray was awarded the Medal of Valor for his actions on this day, an award he took no pleasure in. I asked him to describe the impact that this tragic incident had upon him. He told me that the gun battle hadn't changed him as a person or as a cop, but reinforced the need for preparation. He had added more magazines to his kit, a tactical mirror, a smoke bomb, and Kevlar helmet. He stopped then for a moment and said, "Thank God I didn't do anything wrong. . . . [I] get with training, get in shape, don't eat crap . . . I made the best of it."

It is truly unfortunate that it takes tragedy for peace officers to realize that it is their own responsibility to develop and maintain the habits that will make them victorious, but that is the way it is. They must avoid the luxury of denial—the "it's not going to happen to me" mentality—and be prepared for what "doesn't happen here" to occur.

6

MENTAL CONTROLS IN TACTICAL DECISION MAKING

"USE YOUR HEAD!"

"Use common sense! Think! Use your head!" These phrases are often used with trainees in an attempt to influence them to make better decisions. Good advice, to be sure. In a moment of crisis, however, officers' performance of purposeful and controlled assessment and judgment actions has too often been more difficult to achieve.

When an officer makes a tactical blunder, it's usually not because he or she has too little knowledge of tactical principles and practices. Rather, officers err most often when they do not control the stress of the moment.

Procedural skills and the ability to perform effective mental controls are highly perishable—and degrade rapidly without continuing practice. Previously learned procedures may not be viable in conditions where the officer is faced with a situation he or she has never seen before, where there is no time to prepare for an unanticipated lethal assault against him or her, or where a "no big deal" call for service suddenly turns into a fight for his or her life.

MENTAL CONTROLS FOR TACTICAL DECISION MAKING

Whenever a tragedy occurs that could have been prevented had the involved officer responded differently to a threat, a bitter irony presents itself. I do not believe that it is sufficient to shake our heads and think, *If only they had done it this way instead of that way.* I believe the "why" of self-defeating actions taken by peace officers must become a major part of the discussion.

This relates not just to what went awry tactically, but what happened in the officer's brain that influenced these actions—that is, why an officer trained in the use of tactical principles did not apply them at a moment when they were needed most. It is insufficient to talk about the "winning" or "warrior" mind-set without also providing mental conditioning tools for peace officers to control what their brains and bodies do during severe stress exposure.

A major feature of mental control tools is that their performance under duress activates the complex cognitive (purposeful mental) activities that organize and control behaviors. The tools operate through the brain's capacity to remodel itself and change how it functions in order to adapt to novel or changing conditions (otherwise known as "plasticity").

The actions performed and the experience of using purposeful mental controls when under duress stimulate individuals to react to stress conditions based upon learning, not impulse.

CONTROLLED BREATHING

While it may seem a too-simple idea to some readers, simply taking an intentional, slow, deep breath when under duress is of great benefit to officers for controlling the internal levels of excitation that influence their decision-making. Inhale through the nose while pushing down the stomach. Continue slowly inhaling until the lungs are filled up with air. When the body is filled with air, hold it briefly and then deflate by expelling breath through the mouth. Since adrenaline constricts skeletal muscles, inhaling from the chest instead of the diaphragm will not build up sufficient intra-thoracic pressure to bring excitation levels under the officer's control.

Cardiologist John Kennedy uses the technique of controlled breathing as a means to lower blood pressure in his patients, and recommends using the method as well to lower the levels of stress an individual experiences: "It is within our power to change the way we respond to stress. Using visualization and breathing…people can calm themselves to better their health. You can teach your body how to slow down, how to be present, how to relax. And what this does is it helps you concentrate and protect your heart all at the same time" (Kennedy, 2010).

SWAT training, sniper schools, and tactical instructors have consistently used breathing techniques to slow and stabilize tension levels in operators' bodies to ensure that correct procedures are performed under stress. In the same manner, officers in the field and in institutional settings will benefit from a simple mental control that "resets" and controls the intensity of internal excitation. Controlling the breathing depth and rate while under duress greatly enhances officers' use of the purposeful, concentrated (executive) brain activity that is so necessary to make good decisions under heightened exposure to stress or threat.

The act of concentrating is a critical component of reading the conditions in the environment, assessing the environment for threat, and providing the foundation for making effective decisions. The racing heart rate and excitation that occur during heightened stress or crisis conditions can quickly suppress concentration efforts and influence a rapid transition to action that may well be a distortion or error.

PRIORITIZING SNAPSHOTS

In order to maintain the best possible advantage at a potentially dangerous scene, it is of critical importance, I believe, that officers base their approach and the tactics they choose upon what they see, read, and assess in the here-and-now—and not what they had expected or pre-judged. They must also perform these tasks rapidly enough to take the initiative.

The prioritizing snapshot method involves the officer taking a series of separate, intensive visual-mental "photographs" across the scene, like a laser beam that focuses upon separate, specific pieces of information within the scene to prioritize all the responsibilities or tasks with which the officer is faced. Officers can register a great deal more important information much more quickly when their observation is focused and intentional, rather than just having their attention drawn to what was making the most noise.

The act of prioritizing all areas of responsibility at a scene is an executive mental function that ensures the continued primacy of the "thinking brain"—the parts of the brain that organize the actions the officer is going to take, and which direct their behaviors to accomplish desired goals—while under duress.

Conditioning the mind to automatically prioritize all the separate, important components of a scene or subject prevents perceptual lag, lapses in concentration, "tunnel vision," or delay in their response that result from an individual being startled by the sudden introduction of unanticipated threat, and enables officers to adapt much more rapidly to unanticipated threat conditions. This is what is meant by the term *adaptive expertise*.

SCANNING ACROSS MULTIPLE SENSES

Perception of the world starts in infancy to aid the developing individual to interact more effectively and safely with his or her environment. The infant uses all his or her senses to do so. As individuals grow, however, their experience exposes them to an enormous and potentially overwhelming amount of social and environmental signals and stimuli.

To prevent a sensory overload caused by too much or too intense stimuli in his or her environment, a tendency to narrow the senses when under duress occurs early in the person's life so that his or her perception is limited to safer, more familiar interpersonal and environmental conditions (Lewkowicz, & Ghazanfar, 2009).

Sensory narrowing is a normal, healthy psychological defense that enhances people's ability to control their environment and prevents them from being overwhelmed by too much going on in that environment. When people become police officers, however, the normal tendency for the senses to narrow when they are under duress can be a severe detriment and danger to them.

The narrowing or "tunneling" of perception—as well as the act of disrupting attention, concentration, and decision-making via intense emotion—is a common feature of the human stress response. Prolonged stress exposure and workload have the effect of reducing an officer's capacity to process the information available in the environment: shrinking the area they perceive, scan, and study, and using fewer senses when they do (Baddeley & Hitch, 1994; et al.; Baron, 1986; Broadbent, 1958, 1971; Bundesen, 1990; Bursill, 1958; Cohen, 1980.).

Multisensory scanning provides an effective mental control tool to counter the narrowing or blocking of the senses that occurs during stress exposure. It is accomplished by intentionally broadening and consciously registering all of one's senses—"opening up, seeking out, and reaching for" important features of a scene with every sense—across a 360-degree field.

Scanning across the senses when combined with "prioritizing snapshots" maximizes the amount of information officers will use as they "read," or assess, the immediate situation. This involves consciously grasping the sights and sounds existing at a scene, the smells that are picked up, and how the "hair on the back of one's neck" or "butterflies in the stomach" reacts to the scene.

MANAGING STRESS EXPOSURE
FOR TACTICAL DECISION MAKING

By definition, the act of making decisions about tactics, control options, or strategy requires conscious and goal-directed thinking and judgment. Tactical decision-making involves a sequential thought process in the brain: such as, "What is happening here, has a crime been committed, where is the threat coming from, how imminent and severe is it, where are my positions of best advantage, what force option is required to manage these conditions?" and so forth.

Difficulties in tactical decision making can arise from a number of factors. For example, officers can become "amped up" to the point that they "leap into" a situation with impulsive rather than strategic actions. They may experience shock or become startled because of a sudden introduction of an unexpected threat and have a moment of inaction (the "freeze" part of the "fight or flight" response). Or, as noted earlier, people may form predictions or expectations about what conditions they are about to encounter based upon past experiences. Such as, "Oh, it's going to go this way because it's always happened this way." When those predictions or pre-judgments turn out to be incorrect, the delay created while officers reorient themselves to what they have actually encountered is accompanied by a sense of urgency to "catch up," which overwhelms their thought process.

A short series of "self-talk" questions when approaching a threat or problem can ensure the maintenance of the executive or "thinking brain" during exposure to unanticipated threat or crisis. They are the foundation for effective tactical decision making under stress:

What am I fixing on? What is capturing my attention?

What reaction is this creating in me? That is, a "knot in the gut," the feeling that "something is wrong with this picture."

Why is this important to me?

What do these conditions require regarding force options and tactics?

Do a quick test to confirm my tactics. Will I be putting myself at a disadvantage if I do what my initial impulse compels me to do?

Officers may take for granted the fact that they are excellent observers of information and fact, and don't need to do much in the way of practice to ensure victory for themselves. But they should *not* take for granted the fact that their senses and judgment are going to be functioning at peak levels at the moment they are in a crisis situation. Many officers develop habitual, automatic ways of approaching people, vehicles, or buildings that dull and narrow the senses and thinking without their being aware of it.

"WHAT IS CAPTURING MY ATTENTION?"

To lower the risk of error, injury, or defeat, officers must ensure that their concentration and focus of attention is fixed intently and purposefully upon *this* incident, *here-and-now*—and not upon their memories or expectations that are based in what happened before, or their concerns for critical scrutiny about their actions.

By consciously registering what aspect of the scene or individual is striking the officer as most salient, he or she enacts a purposeful, self-directed mental process that eliminates the risks associated with "head-up-the-ass" approaches to an individual posing threat, or habitual ways of managing situations that are not relevant to the current event.

Several repetitions of intentional self-questioning about what features of the scene are capturing the officer's attention forms mental "blueprints" or "maps" in the brain that automatically register high-priority conditions much more rapidly and under the most difficult and stressful conditions.

Without such conditioning, the officer's response to unexpected threat is much more likely to be instinctive rather than strategic. The risk of hesitation, impulsive behavior, startle, or momentary immobility is then unavoidable.

"WHAT INTERNAL PHYSICAL AND EMOTIONAL REACTIONS IS THIS CONDITION CREATING IN ME?"

Conscious assessment of their internal physical and/or emotional reactions as they approach a subject or scene changes officers' approach from an "automatic pilot," complacent, or "head-up-the-ass" lack of vigilance to one of being alert and self-controlled. This ensures that officers pay attention to the intuitive "red flags" that warn them of impending threat.

A tension in the gut or "hairs standing on the back of the neck" is the brain's way of registering that the officer is in a position of disadvantage. It has retrieved some past memory of a dangerous event triggered by a current condition of threat—before the officer is even aware that the immediate threat is occurring.

The experience of tension (read as "anxiety") and uncertainty is likely to narrow and block the senses, adding to the danger of an officer maintaining tactics that he or she began their approach with but which are no longer viable for encountered conditions.

Too many peace officers develop a habit of blocking or ignoring the internal "signals" that could have prevented a suspect from gaining advantage in a tactical encounter. "All the red flags were there. I saw them, but didn't pay attention to them" is a statement too often uttered by officers who were shot, stabbed, or bludgeoned, or who reacted to threat with instinctive survival behaviors that were found to be out of policy. Pay attention to your instincts—that feeling that is going on in your gut. Make yourself conscious of the internal reaction, then identify what is wrong with a given picture.

"WHY IS THIS IMPORTANT TO ME?"

The act of interpreting why a specific characteristic of the scene or person captured an officer's attention or caused him or her to have a gut reaction activates the part of the brain that retrieves past learning from memory and allows that officer to apply the things that he or she has learned—consciously, intentionally, and immediately—to the current event.

Conscious self-directed narratives create a much clearer picture in officers' minds about what threat they've encountered, how imminent and severe it is, and what they need to do to control the situation—and permits them to organize and direct necessary actions much more rapidly and with greater accuracy. They also greatly enhance officers' memory of the elements of an encounter and their ability to report upon and justify the actions they had to take.

Contemporary police officers cannot avoid moments where their vigilance is dampened or extinguished. As noted earlier, it doesn't take too many times of responding to similar incidents for an officer to approach the scene or individual on an "automatic pilot" or after pre-judging the contact.

QUICK TEST

Performing a quick test of their plan of action causes officers to confirm the propriety of their tactics prior to their "jumping off" into something for which they may be unprepared. It ensures that officers' responses will be strategic rather than impulsive or uncontrolled, and prevents them from placing themselves into positions of disadvantage.

When someone runs from an officer, for example, that officer is highly likely to bolt after them, feeling a compelling sense of urgency to get as close to that person as possible so they can maximize the control they have over the individual. Several instances of officers getting hurt during hot foot pursuits bear witness to the dangers of not confirming one's intended tactics prior to engagement with a dangerous individual. In many cases, suspects' flight behaviors are not attempts to escape arrest, but rather to draw pursuing officers into a trap.

For example, in one incident I responded to many years ago, a suspect jumped several fences and ran through backyards as he fled from a police officer. He suddenly stopped running and hid and waited for the officer to arrive.

The officer was running as fast and as hard as he could. His mind was focused upon one thought—get to this guy and show him the error of his ways. He stopped broadcasting his position to dispatchers and other officers. He exerted no conscious thought about what he was setting himself up for.

The "punch line" of the story is predictable. As soon as the officer's head cleared one fence too many, the suspect shot the officer in the throat. By the grace of God the officer survived and was able to return to work—less likely now to dive headfirst into a swimming pool until he ascertained that there was water in it.

Confirming that your intended tactics will place you in a position of advantage takes little or no time, and its value is incalculable. The immediate elevation in internal levels of excitation causes the executive functions of the brain to be inhibited, and the instinctive "fight or flight" centers to take primacy.

The dampening of the executive brain centers is how peace officers fall prey to emotional capture and the approach trap. They are not thinking or deciding what to do because they have already begun an (usually impulsive) action. The quick test activates those purposeful brain centers at the same time that the officer has begun his or her action. How much is it worth to a peace officer to prevent serious injury, paralysis, or death?

There are, of course, incidents that require an instinctive, immediate response to lethal threat that will depend upon previous training. Getting in the habit of confirming that one's tactics will be the most beneficial will not create a delay during these moments but, instead, result in a more self-regulated response.

ACTS OF WILL, CONCENTRATION, AND MENTAL CONTROL

At its most basic, mental control refers to the ability to influence one's focus of attention by directing it intentionally toward some object. Taking the purposeful act of willing oneself to concentrate upon something specific is the first step toward any other kind of control that people may attain.

Conversely, the brain also suppresses or blocks one's focus of attention as protection. This is a psychological defense against distressing, anxiety-provoking, or overwhelming events. Whether individuals concentrate upon an object or suppress awareness of it is strongly influenced by their feelings. People are unaware of the times that they fail to concentrate upon something because no conscious attention is placed upon it. However, when there is a failure of suppression, there is immediate awareness of it because its failure is accompanied by severe and often anxious emotions (Wegner, 1988).

Examples of failure to suppress a painful memory can be seen in the flashbacks observed in posttraumatic stress disorder (PTSD), where the officer continues to reexperience traumatic moments even though he or she expends substantial effort to suppress those memories.

Conversely, examples of a failure to concentrate can be seen where officers suffered oftentimes catastrophic injury because they ignored the "red flags" that they were walking into an imminent threat. They continued in the manner in which they had begun even though their insides were telling them something was wrong.

"Automatic pilot" work habits are developed as the officer repeatedly encounters highly similar conditions—for example, approaching a vehicle or knowing how someone will behave because he or she has had previous contact with them. Doing things automatically helps make officers more comfortable because their familiarity with the actions taken reduces the level of tension often observed with vigilance.

The conditioned tendency to "stuff" or suppress disturbing or distressing events, emotions, or conditions—for example, the idea that "if I don't think about it and no one sees it, then I don't have a problem"—can weaken officers' ability to read a scene or subject. A habit develops of ignoring and avoiding the "knot in the stomach."

Unfamiliar stimuli are frequently experienced as less pleasing or unpleasant. Where there is conflict between an old expectation and new experience, there is a drive in the individual to reduce the discomfort. This is not a conscious choice. Rather, it is how the mind works in processing information that creates some degree of stress. The brain concentrates upon what is expected, and tends to suppress things that create dissonance, discomfort, or conflict.

The first defense that people are likely to use against conflicted perceptions or expectations is avoidance or denial. We gravitate toward what is familiar, and when dissonance can't be avoided we reconcile differences by favoring what we already know. If new information is not consistent with our habit-formed expectations, we tend to discredit or block it.

We look for agreement with our long-standing beliefs and perceptions (Wegner, 1988). This dynamic is active when officers maintain bad habits that their good luck—not good tactics—has permitted them: "This is how I've always done it. I have more time on the job so I know more than you."

USING VISUALIZATION—THE "WHAT IFS"

It is impossible for training activities to completely replicate the dynamics that an officer may face in a life-threatening encounter. To ensure that they will be maximally prepared to deal with such threat, officers will need to strengthen their capacity to adapt to an unexpected threat. They can build proficiency in adapting to startling or novel events without hesitation, freezing, or impulsive actions through the use of "virtual" practice using visualization and imaging methods.

The mental rehearsal used in creating a scenario of possible events and how an officer is going to act is referred to as the "what ifs" of law enforcement. This is intended to help officers avoid uncertainty and delay in their initial response to encountered threat conditions. But to be effective, the officer doing the visualization or mental rehearsal must be as detailed as possible, registering every sight, sound, smell, or touch that would accompany the visualized condition. The officer should concentrate upon what internal emotion they would be experiencing as he or she approached, for example, unknown threat conditions. He or she should visualize how these senses and feelings would affect the actions they will take to take control of the situation.

It is not sufficient, in my opinion, for officers to visualize some event occurring and say to themselves, "Okay, if this happens, I'll go here, seek cover there," and so on. I believe that officers need to *complete the visualization.* Imagine each and every component and condition of the incident, and perform the tasks that would be necessary for an officer to take even after the most dramatic moment or action is achieved.

The brain will be better prepared to adapt to unanticipated conditions when officers engage in visualizations that take them through all the complex observations, assessments, decisions, and actions from the very beginning to the end. True champions spend more time visualizing what they are going to do in the field of performance than they do actually practicing the skills therein.

7

MANAGEMENT OF STRESS EXPOSURE

WHEN POLICE OFFICERS ARE UNSUCCESSFUL AT CONTROLLING their brains' and bodies' reactions to stress exposure, the impact may be observed in a number of ways: impaired judgment and decision-making; errors in the tactics performed; and degradation of officer health, well-being, and family relationships.

Taking purposeful steps to manage stress exposure when they are enacted *at the exact moment in which the impact of the incident occurs* will inoculate officers against losing the advantage that their training and experience is intended to provide. Intentional self-regulation to lessen reactions to stress exposure also forms a preventive strength with regard to the injuries, illnesses, and personal problems known to affect officers on and off the job.

I believe that every peace officer worth their salt carries some degree of posttraumatic stress "baggage" with them. All this means is that an incident they were not mentally prepared for breached their normal coping resources. Another way to view trauma is to think of a freeze frame where the moment in which the greatest impact of a traumatic incident occurs "locks" in the officer's mind and maintains its impact even though the officer distances him- or herself from the incident in time and space.

The extreme levels of internal physiological excitation and distressed

emotion occurring at the moment the officers were shocked, and the feelings of helplessness they experienced during the incident become "super-
conditioned" in their brain (Pittman & Orr, 1988; van der Kolk et al., 1991).
Thereafter, all components of the officer's reactions to the trauma—not just
the visual memory—become stored in long-term memory.

Instead of providing any real protection and insulation from negative
work stresses, the widely held practice in law enforcement of stuffing emotion—that is, blocking and avoiding any conscious awareness of distressed
emotion—has caused unnecessary injury, sickness, family problems, career
disruption, and death for thousands of peace officers.

THE COSTS OF IGNORING STRESS EXPOSURE EVENTS

Doug had been a police officer for fifteen years. He was a proactive, skilled
officer who was respected by his co-workers and supervisors. He had worked
as a field training officer for three years. He was a big, strong man. He had
won first place in the bench press at the World Police and Fire Games.

He was riding with a trainee who was driving their police vehicle. She
observed a vehicle in a construction zone that had failed to obey a stop sign
that was being held by a worker. Doug told her to pull the vehicle over and
be alert to traffic around her. He remained at the rear of the vehicle they
had stopped so he could observe the vehicle's interior and keep an eye on
his trainee and the driver at the same time. A bulldozer was backing up into
the roadway behind them.

He watched his trainee walk up to the driver's window. The road shoulder that would have allowed the trainee to approach on the passenger's side
was obstructed with construction supplies. This was the last day of her third
phase of field training, and she looked like she was going to be a squared-
away cop when she graduated to fieldwork.

Doug was startled by the sound of a loud crash just behind him. He
turned and saw that a vehicle had tried to pass the bulldozer on the right
to avoid the stoppage, and had slammed into the front blade. Sparks flew
as the vehicle flipped on its side and started spinning toward the trainee.

Everything slowed down then. Doug's vision locked onto the look of surprise and fear on his trainee's face and he watched helplessly as the spinning vehicle struck her and sent her flying into the air. Doug felt as if his feet were buried in cement. He couldn't move as he watched the collision unfold. The trainee landed in a heap and didn't move. In his mind he was watching her die and was mortified that he had done nothing to save her. The trainee regained consciousness on the way to the hospital. She had a number of broken bones and a concussion but, because of her heart and will, would end up returning to work in eight months.

Doug was one of only three officers in the department that did not visit her in the hospital while she began her recovery. He could not bring himself to talk to her because he felt too ashamed. In his mind he was the training officer, and he hadn't prevented her from being harmed—he felt responsible for her injuries.

When she returned to the department a number of months later, he avoided her whenever their paths crossed. What could he say to her? He had done nothing to save her. While he told no one, the image of her body flying through the air and of her dying never went away, even though, in another part of his mind, he knew the actual outcome was different.

Doug resigned from the field training program. He would not risk, as he later termed it, "getting another of my trainees hurt." He never spoke about what he saw as his abject failure. He returned to patrol, quieter now, and was considered withdrawn and aloof by the younger officers on his squad. Months later, he was one of several officers who responded to a domestic disturbance call that went bad.

What had begun as a "no big deal" family disturbance complaint had turned into a hostage situation as a barricaded suspect held his wife and four-year-old daughter at knifepoint. Doug's squad was directed to form a perimeter around the house and hold position until the SWAT and Crisis Negotiation units arrived. He and another officer were positioned near a window at the front of the residence.

They each heard moans and a sucking sound. It sounded like a knife or ax hacking into a melon. They both immediately understood that this situation could not wait—it required action in immediate defense of life. They and another two officers who followed them kicked in the front door and entered the living room.

At first it looked like someone had thrown red paint across the walls and floor like some surreal, abstract painting. Doug was shocked by the amount of blood that could pour out of someone. They got there in time to watch the wife breathe for the last time. It turned out that the blood splatter also came from the suspect's self-inflicted stab wounds. At their command, the suspect dropped the knife and followed its fall to the floor. He, too, died on the way to the hospital. A short house search later, they found the daughter alive, lying in bed with her favorite teddy bear, mute and shaking with terror. The officers stood in awe at the amount of devastation this man had caused.

Doug's department commander told all the involved officers that there were resources being made available for them so that the picture and smell of that house did not remain with them. All the members of the entry team except Doug spoke with the department "shrink." He told the commander, "I don't need the shrink to tell me how f__ked up this was."

He became more isolated from his co-workers. No one in the department knew anything about his personal life. He was as reclusive as one could be while still living among other people. No one knew the pain he carried around with him as an albatross around his neck—no matter how many successful contacts and cases he performed, he had failed to prevent the two most traumatic incidents in his career.

He felt nothing but self-blame, guilt, and anger no matter what he occupied himself with at or away from work. He could not get the false picture of his trainee dying in front of him out of his mind. This picture repeated along with his memory of the sounds and sight of the woman dying after she was stabbed so many times. Each time they recurred, the memories were accompanied by depression and self-directed anger at his failures. It was as if he were watching a horror movie that he starred in as the person who fails to save the victim—a movie that played over and over.

Then one day, Doug was the first responding officer to a disturbance call involving a fight at a local bar. When he arrived, he saw several young men standing over a young male who was writhing on the ground. A pool of blood was spreading from underneath the male, who turned out to be the victim of a stabbing by another male who had fled before Doug got there.

When Doug leaned down to talk to the victim, the individual grabbed onto his arms and began to plead with him: "Please, officer, please don't let me die. Please help me. Don't let me die here. I don't want to die." Doug kept hold of the stabbing victim. He assured the young man that paramedics were en route and would take care of him.

Shortly after Doug made this comment to the victim, the man's eyes rolled back in his head and he died. This was the last straw. Doug broke down. He started sobbing there in the bar, holding the dead body in his arms. He couldn't stop sobbing, even when fellow officers and paramedics arrived to transport the victim.

His sergeant telephoned and asked me to talk with Doug. He told me that Doug appeared to be having some kind of breakdown. Doug had experienced the worst possible thing that could happen to a peace officer. At a moment where they urgently needed to impact the conditions they had encountered, there was absolutely nothing they could do—they had been helpless.

Because stress exposure affects both the physiology and psychology of officers, both the mind and body must be consistently challenged. The antidote to feelings of helplessness is a process of engaging in purposeful acts of will that stretch and empower them—actions that are incompatible with feelings of helplessness.

While getting stronger was a necessary step for Doug to take, he could not face going to the gym to work out because he started to well up with emotion and become tearful when other people saw him. He was humiliated, "especially because I was such an asshole to other cops who got screwed up in police work."

He was unable to stop crying whenever he began to speak about the incidents described above and, because becoming physically stronger and more powerful was a major part of his treatment, he was assigned the task of climbing the tall, steep hill behind his house from the bottom, carrying a heavy stone until he could make it to the top.

The purpose for this unusual means of treatment was quite similar to the moral in the myth of Sisyphus, a man whom the gods punished by dooming him to push a boulder up the side of a hill forever, only for it to roll back to the bottom each time. Sisyphus' situation is tragic, because he knows his fate. At the same time, however, the insight he achieves with this understanding also places him above his fate.

It did not matter how many times Doug had to stop and put the stone down on the ground to rest. He simply had to pick it up again to his chest and continue climbing. I told him that he had to perform this part of his treatment because verbal therapy by itself just wasn't cutting it.

He began the process of trying to reach the top of the hill carrying the round, 160-pound stone. After the early "baby steps" on the path to progress, he began to feel a sense of achievement as he saw himself improve in strength and stamina. The feeling that he was less weakened than before—even though he still felt grief and guilt—transferred to other parts of his life and he felt more able to talk about what had happened to him. He finally acknowledged the damage he had done to himself by blaming himself for things he had no possible way to impact.

His repeated efforts over a number of weeks literally rewired his brain. He went from viewing himself as a helpless and hopeless defeated person to one who now recognized that he again had the ability to overcome obstacles in his path. And that is the whole point of physical, mental, and emotional fitness conditioning.

Once an officer has been seriously affected by his or her exposure to a distressing, disturbing, or traumatic incident (e.g., witness to child murders and abuse; witness to an elderly person's head bashed in from a bat by her deranged son while she slept; witness to innocent victims of fatal collisions that resemble officers' family members; victim of suicide-by-cop), it is more difficult—but not impossible—to extinguish the potentially damaging changes that occur in his or her brain, body, and family and/or personal life.

CHANGING THE BRAIN

Police officers possess a capability that has been completely ignored in their training and education—one that can literally save their lives in tactical situations as well as insulate them from many harmful effects of stress expo-sure—namely, resilience. With continued repetitions of a new, purposeful action, new nerve cells and new nerve connections (i.e., blueprints for a response) grow in the brain as the action becomes conditioned.

London taxi drivers are made to take a test to prove that they possess expert knowledge of the entirety of city streets, avenues, places of interest, et cetera. The brain size of a group of new drivers was studied with com-puter-aided imagery before they began to study and then again after they passed the examination they needed to obtain their licenses. The parts of their brain that receive, process, retain, and remember the facts they studied and learned had become significantly larger (Arden & Linford, 2009).

Research has proven that the brain is flexible: it has "plasticity" and thus can be changed to form new, more adaptive thoughts, emotions, and actions that, once conditioned, can become part of a new emotional response to stress exposure (Arden & Linscome, 2010).

The fact that the brain possesses plasticity has profound implications for how peace officers maintain mental and behavioral control during and after severe stress exposure and organizational dysfunction. Engaging in pur-poseful proactive actions and thought simultaneous to a confrontation with an ugly scene enables officers to turn feelings of helplessness into a plan to engage in actions that create better feelings after they are done—instead of these moments turning into prolonged, toxic stress reactions where they become part of the individual's emotional being.

Sometimes the cop brings ugly feelings home with which they do not know how to deal—whether they were created in the field, the institu-tion, or the organization itself—and dumps them on his or her family by withdrawing into isolation, or showers his or her family with "short-fused," impatient reactions that create distress in his or her home life.

In other cases, officers handle the stresses of the job quite well, have no negative moods, thoughts, or emotions, and have a great family life; but develop irregular heartbeat, high blood pressure, coronary disease, digestive disorders, diabetes, or other diseases after about twenty years on the job (Blum, 1998; Violanti et al., 1988).

Younger officers usually don't see the need to actively manage their internal reactions to work stress exposure because, for the first fifteen years or so, they are healthier than most adult workers (Violanti et al., 1988). After that time, their unmanaged exposure to work stresses accumulates and eventually creates the proverbial "straw that breaks the camel's back." After about nineteen years of service, the morbidity and mortality rates for peace officers elevate rapidly—well beyond those for civilian municipal, county, and state workers (Violanti et al., 1988).

Cumulative and posttraumatic stress reactions often occur because officers are not provided with skill proficiency in the use of the *accessible* control tools needed to counteract the toxic parts of their work. When officers are able to respond to an ugly scene or situation with immediate self-regulation that dissipates or defuses the harmful elements, there is much less chance of them carrying the ugliness away with them as they gain distance from the scene.

The steps to manage intense stress exposure must begin with officers changing their tradition of ignoring and avoiding distressing or disturbing reactions to traumatic events. Rather than "stuffing them," peace officers must do better, I believe, at consciously processing unpleasant internal reactions to events at the moment that they occur. They don't need to show it; just feel the pain, acknowledge that it's there, take steps to lower levels of internal (mental, physical, and emotional) agitation, and then counter its impact with strong and purposeful acts of will.

TURNING DOWN THE HEAT

When events that officers confront contain conditions that elicit a strong emotional reaction, their conscious awareness of those events are accompanied by powerful physiological and hormonal reactions in their brain and body. The brain then encodes—within twenty to thirty seconds—all the different reactions the officer is having to the event and stores them in long-term memory.

Long-term memory operates at a mostly unconscious level in the brain. Once there, an event that triggered a powerful, distressed reaction continues to impact officers without them being aware of the source of toxic reactions in their brain and body. Emotion-arousing events are more likely to be remembered over a long period of time, both because the event holds a personal meaning for the individual and because these events create powerful physiological reactions that further reinforce their storage in the officers' long-term memory (Adolphs, 1999).

Ugly events create ugly feelings. So it is logical that the officer would feel acutely uncomfortable or distressed emotions when these events occur. Problems develop, however, because police officers have a tendency to blame and criticize themselves for being unable to impact the event the way they urgently felt the need to.

I have found that peace officers interpret their bad feelings about something they were helpless to prevent as defeat, "screwing up," or failure. This tendency will exacerbate the severity of the event's impact upon the officer, which is then stored as a long-term memory. Self-directed criticism is founded upon law enforcement's demand that officers never fail to control the situation and themselves. So if they do have a distressing or disturbing feeling that is logical and normally experienced after an ugly event, their interpretation of that feeling is that "it must mean I screwed up—otherwise I wouldn't feel this way."

Traumatic memories trigger the activity of the survival-oriented anxiety/fear centers in officers' brains. While the fear response is adaptive in mobilizing an individual to cope with impending threat, it also has a downside. LeDoux (2002) showed that the amygdala—the part of the brain that initiates the anxiety/fear response—could be conditioned to elicit a fear response when there is no reason to do so.

However, it was also shown that activation of the parts of the brain that engage in purposeful thoughts and functioning exerts a mediating or dampening effect upon the brain's anxiety/fear centers. In other words, engaging in purposeful thinking and self-empowering actions in the presence of anxiety or fear dampens and lessens the frequency, severity, and duration of these emotions (LeDoux, 2002).

Therefore, when officers are aware that some event creates a powerful reactive response in them, they should engage in mental and physical controls *at that very moment* with an intent to counter its impact. Then, when the event is transferred to long-term, largely unconscious memory, the damaging and/or disturbing elements of the event are lessened in severity—less able to exert prolonged disturbance or damage to the officer.

SLOW AND DEEP BREATHING

As noted earlier, the slow, deep breathing—inhaling through the nose while pushing the belly down until the trunk chamber is filled with air, holding it a split second to create intra-thoracic pressure, and then expelling the breath with some degree of strength through pursed lips—that enhances tactical decision-making by lowering the heart rate also benefits officers by lessening the intensity of internal arousal when performed at the moment the exposure to stress occurs.

COMPETITIVE IMAGING

Thoughts, visions, and memories of traumatic events are accompanied by an often extreme, distressing emotional state. Because of their extreme emotional character, the memory of such events recurs in a continuing, intrusive manner even though the individual expends substantial effort not to think about them.

Experiencing such memories causes feelings of helplessness and hopelessness because the officer is unable to remove them from consciousness. The traditional methods of ignoring and denying distressing emotions don't work. The moment in time that had the greatest impact upon officers is locked in their minds. Their brains are in a transient shock condition and cease to process the experience in the way it normally would with less traumatic conditions.

Competitive imaging is the act of concentrating intensely—with each sense being consciously focused on recalling a very positive memory, place, or event—one that created relaxation and happiness for the person. The deliberate retrieval of positive memories produces a more comfortable response that is incompatible with the anxiety created by disturbing memories.

This is not just "thinking happy thoughts." Every sense has memory. Competitive imaging works by having the officer intentionally and intensely focusing his or her attention upon recollection of sights, sounds, smells, taste, and feel of events, places, or individuals that created happiness and contented feelings in their past.

The method is intended to provide psychological "first aid" to peace officers involved in traumatic incidents—and to initiate the growth of new nerve cells and nerve connections (think of them as mental blueprints that become habits) that are predisposed to lessen the harmful impact of a work encounter. When they concentrate strongly upon "safe places" where they experienced positive feelings, the severity of the traumatic moment is temporarily lessened. The act contributes to officers activating their "thinking" brain, the part that enables them to organize and direct their behaviors to empower themselves: to counteract helpless feelings that accompanied the trauma.

THE DEVELOPMENT OF EMOTIONAL RESILIENCE

One of the most common reactions to stress exposure in police officers is a loss of vigor and feelings of vitality in the aftermath of ugly events. Many officers reported to me that they had stopped their usual activities and contact with people (especially loved ones) that previously brought pleasure to them, because they "just did not have the energy to do them" or "just felt lousy."

As noted earlier, what we do or experience every day becomes familiar to us. The brain perceives what is familiar and habituates to it—that is, forms nerve connections that increase the likelihood that the thought, emotion, or action will occur again and again with less intensity needed to initiate it. To lessen the strength and intensity of negative conditioning to reactions that come from ugly events, officers will intentionally need to alter their psychological and physiological condition on a habitual basis.

In the aftermath of an officer-involved shooting, for example, officers are usually given a few days off on paid administrative leave. This is the time that they should be taking a trip, going for hikes in the outdoors and, of most importance, engaging in physical conditioning that "sweats out" the toxic residues of the event over a more prolonged period than is normally performed.

Staying at home and recounting the incident to all of the friends and co-workers who telephone them will only maintain the effects of the event upon them and increase the likelihood that those effects will remain with them in long-term memory. Since the brain rapidly habituates to repeated conditions, officers should be altering—that is, defusing—the levels of internal excitation in the immediate aftermath of a traumatic event just like an oscillating wavelength constantly changes the intensity of the wave.

In a similar manner, officers should, in my opinion, follow the events they confront at work with purposeful activities that, once performed, leave them in a more relaxed, happier condition—that is, activities that counteract ugly experiences at work and replace them with more positive situations. Taking control over their experiences and activities will strongly influence officers' ability to remove themselves from the disturbing or damaging psychological and physiological environments to which they are exposed in the course of their work.

I have often been told by peace officers, "I leave work at work." Does that mean that they defuse the internal excitation and arousal occurring at work, and remove themselves from the cop role and self-image to become loving fathers, mothers, and life partners? Very often, unfortunately, officers carry into their home life the "baggage" of their work experiences without being aware of it.

DON'T WASTE THE GIFT

Most of the peace officers with whom I have spoken over the years had no clue about how to celebrate the good things they had in their lives. It was as if they took the good things for granted—that is, didn't pay much attention to them—and their attention was focused instead upon things that frustrated or disturbed them.

I have taken care of peace officers whose children died from cancer and who accidentally caused the death of children in collisions or by unintended firearm discharge. I learned from these experiences not to take any good things in my life for granted because I have seen how quickly good things can be taken away. I came to understand and concentrate upon the fact that every day that my wife and children don't have cancer or another fatal disease is a miracle. Every time they avoid being a victim of violence and tragedy is a cause for celebration.

The choice is simple: maintain acts, thoughts, and feelings that are celebrations of the good things in your life, or possess only the frustrations and tragedies that occur on a daily basis in law enforcement. You have to fight for the happiness you're going to get in this profession. It doesn't come by itself.

The changes in brain activity that are brought about by actions that stretch officer capabilities in physical training, hobbies, and family relationships act as an antidote for the negative consequences of stress exposure. Relaxation achieved in enjoyable hobbies is incompatible with anxiety. The activity relaxes them and removes them from the psychological environment of law enforcement; and the anxiety, worry, and depression centers of the brain are inhibited.

Activities that empower the self are incompatible with feelings of depression. Police depression is caused most often by feelings of helplessness or loss. Therefore, activities that are empowering to officers in mind and body similarly counteract the variety of toxic reactions to stress exposure (e.g., physical illness, depression of mood, withdrawal from loved ones, etc.) that would otherwise develop.

Over time, as officers stop the self-defeating habit of avoiding and ignoring internally occurring emotions, and as they apply personal controls and habits that oppose the ugliness of negative experiences and organizational dysfunction they encounter with empowering acts of will, they will substantially lower the amount of brain activity that precipitates or maintains upset and difficulties in their lives.

8

RETHINKING THE PRIORITIES

CONFIDENCE CAN BE MISPLACED

Someone who is confident of his or her strength and athleticism will, when confronted with an unexpected threat, likely initiate a physical response to regain advantage over a foe. The immediate, impulsive actions that are sometimes undertaken in hot foot and vehicle pursuits are driven by the confident feeling of certainty that officers possess of themselves and of those who would attempt to evade them; a view that "You will submit to me or I will take you down."

Officers must believe in their power and strength, because it is through their use that they develop their "edge" of self-confidence—a critically important trait when attempting to overcome assaults against them. But, in addition to strength and power, officers must also ensure that they use effective judgment in how they approach dangerous conditions. It is difficult to do so, either when the officer is focusing his or her attention upon circumstances that are outside the tactical encounter (such as preoccupation with the scrutiny they expect) instead of the dangers that could prevent them from going home; or, when faced with unexpected threat, return to actions that had always worked before but are not sufficient to overcome the danger that confronts them now.

THROUGH NO FAULT OF THEIR OWN

On November 29, 2009, Richard Clemmons, a thirty-seven-year-old male African American, murdered four police officers in Washington state. The after-action report produced by Assistant Chief Mike Zaro (Lakewood Police Department, Pierce County, Washington) reported that Clemmons had a history of incarceration for violent offenses, had recently been involved in a physical altercation with local sheriff's deputies, and had been released on bail from his arrest for assault and raping a child on November 23. Clemmons stood at five-foot seven inches and weighed 208 pounds.

He had begun making threats on November 26 to friends and family that he was going to kill police officers and innocent citizens. He removed the bail bond company's GPS tracking device from his body on the same date. Members of his family and friends reported that he was becoming increasingly irrational on November 27 and 28, that he was carrying two guns, and had repeated his threats to kill people.

He entered a coffee shop early in the morning that was often frequented by area police officers. Without warning or hesitation, he executed a female officer by shooting her in the back of her head. Her sergeant had less than one second to react. Clemmons turned to him and shot him in the head. Both officers died instantly. Then he killed the two other officers who were standing at the front counter waiting for their order to be filled.

The four police officers had just concluded an early morning incident that involved a violent physical altercation with a mentally disordered person who'd been under the influence of drugs. Afterward, they went to a coffee shop that was a familiar setting to them, to relax after a tough situation. Excerpts taken from the 2011 after-action report, used with permission from assistant chief Mike Zaro of the Lakewood Police Department, describe how the incident occurred:

Clemmons entered the shop and was verbally greeted by the barista helping Officer _____ (the third police officer murdered). Clemmons did not reply and walked . . . directly to the tables where two officers were sitting. He turned, produced a nine millimeter semiautomatic Glock, and shot Officer _____ in the back of the head, killing her instantly. Clemmons then turned and shot Sgt. _____ in the right side of the head, killing him instantly. Evidence indicated the Glock malfunctioned after the second shot and was no longer capable of firing. After the second shot and with Clemmons' semiautomatic now inoperable, Officer _____ closed distance on Clemmons and became engaged in a physical altercation. During this altercation Clemmons produced a .38 caliber revolver and shot Officer _____ in the head, killing him near instantly. Officer _____ [the fourth officer murdered], who had also closed [the] distance on Clemmons but started much further away than Officer _____, continued in the physical confrontation with Clemmons.

During the struggle with Officer _____, Clemmons fired the .38 revolver multiple times, striking various surfaces in different directions in the shop, eventually expending all the rounds in the pistol. During the struggle, Officer _____'s taser and taser holster were removed from his belt. The removal of both the holster and the taser indicate it was torn from his belt as opposed to being drawn. Further into the altercation, Officer _____'s duty weapon, a .40 caliber Glock, was removed from his holster. Officer _____ shot Clemmons once in the torso—a nonfatal wound. Clemmons eventually gained control of the pistol and shot Officer _____ in the head, killing him instantly; Officer _____ fell to the ground in the threshold of the front door. Clemmons then fled the scene on foot to his awaiting truck and getaway driver approximately .2 miles away, leaving the two guns he came with behind in the shop and taking Officer _____'s gun with him.

There was nothing that the first two officers could have done to predict that someone intent upon murder would walk into a coffee shop filled with cops at 7:30 in the morning and shoot them without warning. After all, as the report pointed out:

The officers were not in the middle of any enforcement action; they were in a familiar public place with frequent traffic and multiple officers facing each direction to visually cover the entire shop. Finally, we looked at the actions of each officer. Officer _____ had no warning and no time to react to a threat prior to being shot. Sgt. _____ would have heard and seen the shot that killed Officer _____ but would have had less than

1.5 seconds to see the gun, recognize the shot, and react prior to being shot himself. Officer _____ would have seen and heard both shots and his reaction was to close the distance and physically engage Clemmons.

The officers who were the third and fourth to be killed closed in on the suspect and engaged him physically. Their immediate response to the shocking events that were unfolding, instead of drawing their firearms and shooting him to extinguish the threat, were to engage him with their hands—i.e., less than lethal levels of force. The investigators of the incident speculated, "One likely explanation can be found in Officer _____'s background: He was athletic and very strong. During a violent encounter, most of us will revert to what we know best and what has worked best for us in the past, whether it is impact weapons, tasers, firearms, or physical ability."

In other words, many officers, in the heat of the moment, revert to actions with which they are familiar and comfortable *without making a conscious decision to do so*. As noted earlier, familiarity brings with it comfort, and with comfort comes a relaxing of tension and vigilance.

When they are ambushed, many officers experience intense, momentary shock and disbelief that "this is not supposed to happen—they are supposed to run and I'm supposed to chase and catch them, not the other way around." It is at this moment—when officers experience shock or uncertainty—that habitual, reflex, and sometimes self-defeating behaviors are most likely.

The four police officer victims had felt the need to defuse the arousal and tensions they had experienced in the physical altercation they'd had earlier. They accordingly and logically lessened the amount of acute, focused concentration that had existed at the earlier stressful scene as a part of their efforts at relaxing. Their expectations about the experience they were about to undergo in buying coffee and sitting down would not be predictive of a great deal of threat.

"You can't expect peace officers to maintain their vigilance all the time—it would drive them and everyone near them crazy," is a refrain I have heard throughout my career. This is not to suggest that peace officers should constantly live with hyper-vigilance. But the fact is that officers are quick to create expectations about what their environment poses for them as a means of reducing tension. And expectations that turn out to be inaccurate predictors of the encounter become highly toxic to officers. They create a moment of startle or shock that compromises their ability to adapt to the actual threat conditions.

To expend energy and resources to teach police officers tactical procedures without teaching—and practicing—mental and emotional controls over what their brains and bodies do in a moment of unexpected crisis is insufficient. Proficiency at controlling managing officers' mental and physiological response to unexpected threat is rarely at the forefront of law enforcement training. This lack of attention to the peace officer's psychology during moments of unexpected crisis cannot help but cause more injury to those who serve.

Several studies were referenced in this book that document the perceptual and behavioral changes that occur as a result of officers' exposure to moments of high stress or crisis. For example, an article by Captain Quinn McCarthy of the Tucson Police Department discussed the importance of the management of stress exposure in adapting to an unexpected threat:

The officers did exactly what their training expected of them. Learned tactics—whether appropriate or not—become the selected course of action and will be pursued come hell or high water. While it can be desirable to rely on conditioned training, it is not acceptable for that conditioning to be void of thought. This applies to both tactical situations and non-tactical situations alike. The concept of "adaptive expertise"—the ability to adapt to changing conditions with no loss of mental accuracy or tactical proficiency—needs to become the cornerstone of training programs. Training an officer to *think* is more than just telling him or her to have some common sense. It most definitely goes further than the frequently used means to teach tactical thinking by providing officers with a myriad of tactical "tools in the toolbox." Tactical thinking under stress training requires an emphasis on conditioning an officer to think through the situation with purposeful actions based upon the circumstances the officer is faced with or those that are suddenly, unexpectedly introduced into the incident. The sad fact is that despite some very well intentioned training programs, they have in fact created situations where officers performed in the field exactly as they did in training, leading directly to unnecessary injuries and deaths. General

Al Gray, Commandant United States Marine Corp, stated it best when he said, 'Tactics is not *whether* you go left or right. Tactics is *why* you go left or right.'" (McCarthy, 2012)

Too many police officers have been shot and killed with their weapons still holstered. They saw the threat develop visually but, for whatever reason, did not adapt their tactical response in time or with sufficient force to manage the rapidly changing and unanticipated conditions they were either too slow or too reticent to handle. Their training and experience, while clearly effective prior to these events, did not prepare them to maintain an intense, focused presence of mind that would permit them to "do the right thing" faster than the suspect who was intent upon causing them harm.

Many officers have told me that "I wouldn't let that happen to me." They expressed certainty that they would take immediate and decisive action (referring to their use of lethal force) to extinguish the threat. But until you practice—under duress—the exact behaviors necessary to prevent a startled reaction from compromising your safety, you shouldn't be so quick to think, "I can take care of whatever comes at me."

Law enforcement's reluctance to sponsor continuing practice in ground fighting, sparring, and other forms of defense—because of fears that claims for injury on duty will occur—will decrease some officers' confidence in their ability to combat severe assault against them. Combining the above with political and administrative pressures that threaten criticism and/or punishment for using serious force creates an environment in which more officers will delay, hesitate, or experience a preoccupation with scrutiny concerns instead of reacting decisively and immediately to threat.

The mental and emotional well-being of officers is most often considered as the "domain of the weak." And yet it is within the psychology and mind of the officer that determines whether they make it through a work shift without getting seriously wounded, injured, or killed. Maintaining the well-being of one's career, family relationships, and long-term health are subjects too rarely emphasized in training, supervision, and discussion.

Lack of attention to these critical components of a person's life have too often resulted in peace officers' lives being ruined or lost. In one moderate-size Southern California police department alone, for example, seven officers' strategies for dealing with stress resulted in their arrest for driving under the influence of alcohol in a single year, with one of them arrested for the third time for the same offense.

When they experience feelings of helplessness and/or defeat in an incident or organizational difficulty, officers can, without realizing it, begin to compensate for these feelings by engaging in self-defeating and/or self-destructive behaviors, including withdrawal from loved ones, ceasing physical and mental conditioning activities, preoccupation or distraction or "head up the ass" mentality when approaching a suspect, suicide, shoplifting, driving three hundred miles to Las Vegas on a lark in a marked police vehicle while on duty, or inappropriate involvement with informants or street people.

After years of dedicating yourself to the protection and safety of the community you serve, what should be the fruits of your labor? Police officers put their life and health in jeopardy every day for people they don't even know. And yet, with minimal attention paid by many in law enforcement to their health and well-being, too many respond to the conditions they encounter in those duties with toxic and/or self-defeating actions.

The reality is that today's police officers must wade through a great deal of decision-making regarding the law and case decisions in determining whether they have cause to control or detain a non-compliant or assaultive individual. The avoidance of liability for them and the jurisdictions they serve demands that they do so.

But in order to do so, they must be capable of maintaining their presence of mind in the immediate aftermath of some condition that may have startled or shocked them. Officers must, I believe, take the responsibility to train, practice, and prepare themselves to maintain intentional thoughts, physical and emotional reactions, and tactical actions so that they may be performed at peak levels under duress.

In this age of video capability in every phone-wielder's hands, every law enforcement encounter is likely to be taped and listed on YouTube. Uses of force are not pretty. Officers cannot help but be influenced to some extent by their concerns that they could be the next officer sacrificed to media frenzy should they apply the levels of force that coincide with the levels (and type) of suspect/subject threat with which they are confronted.

"Do the job without error or complaint, or get out of the business" has been the primary message to new recruits when it comes to a discussion of their mental and emotional health. The feeling is, for the most part, that peace officers are provided with training and knowledge in the procedures and practices they will need to use in the field, so they should be held accountable to perform those skills without error, liability, or loss—no matter how severe or unexpected the event may be.

What, then, should peace officers hold *themselves* accountable for? How many of America's finest must be lost before they fundamentally change their priorities—from avoiding the realities of the impact that their work exerts upon their inner being to the quest for mastery that brings victory in law enforcement?

The primary point of this book is that victory cannot be gained solely through an officer's knowledge of tactical principles. While some in law enforcement naturally and instinctively manage unexpected or rapidly changing threat conditions without delay or error, many contemporary police officers are, I fear, less likely to seize immediate control of a resistive, assaultive, or disturbed individual. This can be either from a fear of consequences to them, locking themselves into a verbal control option that is no longer viable, immediate performance of habits of which they are confident but which are not appropriate for the current encounter; or a personal reluctance to use physical force even when their assessment of the condition with which they are faced calls for decisive physical controls performed at the earliest possible moment.

When peace officers drive themselves toward excellence and mastery in all parts of their lives, they are much more likely to respond effectively to an unexpected threat than are those who find "just okay" good enough, or those who do not expend substantial and continued effort to prepare themselves for the worst-case scenario. Officers who do drive themselves on the quest for mastery in their lives and work will make the correct decisions and do the right things during a moment of crisis because they have conditioned their minds, bodies, and skills to overcome every obstacle in their path— and adapt to unexpected threat encounters without any degradation that could arise from uncontrolled officer reactions to startle or shock.

It is my hope that readers will practice the mental, emotional, and behavioral control tools discussed in this book, as well as learn other tools to maintain their well-being and chances for victory from as many sources as possible. New recruits entering law enforcement are bombarded with the many ways in which they can lose their home, life savings, or freedom. They receive field training from officers, but are not guided thereafter through experiences their life may not have prepared them for. From whom will they be influenced the most?

There are a number of officers in every law enforcement agency who are the agency's informal leaders. They have street or institutional credibility with all members of the department. Should the strength of character, wisdom, and ability that brought these leaders the respect of others be wasted?

These officers have developed effective strategies to work through the law enforcement system in a manner that brought them success. They possess tactical expertise as well as skills in managing the stresses that come with the job. Incoming officers will develop values, attitudes, and response tendencies whether or not there is a positive mentoring system within the organization to help guide them to do the right thing when it counts. But mentoring programs are, in fact, needed to enhance the viability of one's passage through their law enforcement career.

The will to survive and the strength and ability to do so are precious and perishable commodities. They are achieved through hundreds of hours of preparation, training, and practice by officers in the skills necessary to overcome individuals who are intent upon taking their lives.

There is always someone out there who is disturbed or assaultive, bigger and stronger than the officer, and may further have the advantage of military tactical experience. The individual who is most prepared at a given moment to adapt to the encountered threat and achieve peak performance with his or her response will be the victor. The combination of active, focused attention upon the task at hand, mental and physical self-regulation, acts of will, and maximal effort cannot lead to defeat.

REFERENCES

Adolphs, R. (1999). Social cognition and the human brain. *Trends in Cognitive Sciences* 3, 469–479.

Arden & Linford (2009). Brain-based therapy with adults. New Jersey: John Wiley & Sons.

Axelrod, J., & Reisine, T. (1984). Stress hormones. *Science*, 224, 452–459.

Baddeley, A. D., & Hitch, G. J. (1994). Developments in the concept of working memory. *Neuropsychology*, 8(4), 485–493.

Baron, R. S. (1986). Distraction-conflict theory: Progress and problems. In L. Berkowitz (Ed.), *Advances in experimental social psychology* (pp. 1–40). New York: Academic Press.

Baumann, J., & DeSteno, D. (2010, October). Emotion guided threat detection: Expecting guns where there are none. *Journal of Personality and Social Psychology, 99*(4), 595–610.

Blum, L (2000). *Force under pressure: How cops live and why they die.* New York: Lantern Books.

Bransford, J.; Brown, A.; Cocking, R. (Eds.).(2000). *How people learn: Brain, mind, experience, and school, commission on behavioral and social sciences and education.* Washington, D.C.: National Research Council, National Academy Press.

Broadbent, D. E. (1958). *Perception and communication.* London: Pergamon.

Broadbent, D. E. (1971). *Decision and stress.* London: Academic Press.

Bundesen, C. (1990). A theory of visual attention. *Psychological Review, 97*, 523–547.

Bursill, A. E. (1958). The restriction of peripheral vision during exposure to hot and humid conditions. *Quarterly Journal of Experimental Psychology, 10,* 113–129.

California Commission on Police Officer Standards and Training. (1996). Law enforcement officers killed and assaulted.

Cannon-Bowers, J.A. & Salas, E. (Eds.) (1998). Making decisions under stress: Implications for individual and team training. Washington, D.C.: American Psychological Association Books.

Chi, M.; Glaser, R., & Farr, M. J. (Eds.). (1988). The nature of expertise. Hillsdale, Ill.: Lawrence Erlbaum.

Cohen, J. L. (1980). Social facilitation: Audience versus evaluation apprehension effects. *Motivation and Emotion, 4*(1), 21–34.

Crawford, V., Schlager, M., Toyama, Y., Riel, M., & Vahey, P. (2005). "Characterizing adaptive expertise in science reaching." Paper presented at the American Educational Research Association Annual Conference. April 11–15, Montreal, Canada.

Engel, G. L. (1971). Sudden and rapid death during psychological distress. *Annals of Internal Medicine, 74,* 771–782.

Federal Bureau of Investigation. (2007). Law enforcement officers killed and assaulted. Uniform Crime Statistics.

Federal Bureau of Investigation. (2009). Law enforcement officers killed and assaulted. Uniform Crime Reports.

Gellhorn, E. (1968). Central nervous system tuning and its implications for neuropsychiatry. *Journal of Nervous and Mental Disease, 147,* 148–162.

Gray, J. (1985). Issues in the neuropsychology of anxiety. In A. Tuma & J. Maser (Ed.), *Anxiety and Anxiety Disorders* (pp. 5–26). Hillsdale, Ill.: Lawrence Erlbaum.

Grossman, D. (1995). *On killing: The psychological cost of learning to kill in war and society.* New York: Little, Brown.

Janis, I., & Mann, L. (1977). *Decision making.* New York: Free Press.

Janis, I., Defares, P., & Grossman, P. (1983). Hypervigilant reactions to threat. In H. Selye (Ed.), *Selye's Guide to Stress Research* (Vol. 3, pp. 1–42). New York: Van Nostrand Reinhold.

Johnson, J. (2010). Force and the fatigue threshold: The point of no return, (6). AELE Mo. L. J. 501 Special Articles Section, June.

Keinan, G. (1987). Decision making under stress: Scanning of alternatives under controllable and uncontrollable threats. *Journal of Personality and Social Psychology, 52*, 639–644.

Keinan, G. (1988). Training for dangerous task performance: The effects of expectations and feedback. *Journal of Applied Social Psychology, 18*, 355–373.

Kennedy, J. (2010). *The 15 minute heart*. New York: John Wiley & Sons.

Kolb, L. C. (1987). A neuropsychological hypothesis explaining post traumatic stress disorders. *American Journal of Psychiatry, 144*, 989–995.

LeDoux, J. (1996). *The emotional brain*. New York: Touchstone.

Lehner, P., Seyed-Solorforough, M., O'Connor, M. F., Sak, S., & Mullin, T. (1997). Cognitive biases and time stress in team decision making. IEEE *Transactions on Systems, Man, & Cybernetics Part A: Systems & Humans, 27*, 698–703.

Lewinski, William, & Vickers, Joan, Journal of Human Movement Science, Volume 31, Issue 1, February, 2012.

Lewinski, W. (2007-2011). *Force Science Institute Newsletter*.

Lewkowicz, D., & Ghazanfar, A. (2009, September 11). The emergence of multisensory systems through perceptual narrowing. *Trends in Cognitive Sciences, 13*, (11), 470–478.

Lubbock Avalanche-Journal, Lubbock, Texas. (2000, August).

Luttrell, M., & Robinson, P. (2007). *Lone survivor: The eyewitness account of Operation Redwing and the lost heroes of SEAL Team 10*. New York: Little, Brown, & Co.

McCarthy Q. (2012). Police leadership: A primer for the individual and the organization. New York: Palgrave McMillan.

Myer, G. (2010, July). The BART shooting tragedy: Lessons to be learned. *Police One*.

Oatley, K., Keltner, D., & Jenkins, J. (2006). *Understanding emotions* (Second Ed.). Malden, Mass.: Blackwell Publishing.

Ochs, E., & Capps, L. Narrating the self. (1996). *Annual Review of Anthropology, . 25*, 19–43.

Office of Communications and Public Liaison. (2010, May). National Institute of Neurological Disorders and Stroke, National Institutes of Health, Bethesda, Md.

Orr, S. P., Pitman, R. K., Lasko, N., & Herz, L. R. (1993). Psychophysi-
ological assessment of posttraumatic stress disorder imagery in World
War II and Korean combat veterans. *Journal of Abnormal Psychology. 102*,
152–159.

Rodionov, A. (2005, December). Mental conditioning before the game.
FIBA Assist Magazine, 4(8), 35–36.

Staw, R. M., Sandelands, L .E., & Dutton, J. E. (1981). Threat-rigidity
effects in organizational behavior: A multi-level analysis. *Administrative
Science Quarterly, 26*, 501–524.

Texas Department of Public Safety. (2000, September). Chapparal Newsletter.

van der Kolk, B., Greenberg, M., Boyd, H., & Krystal, J. (1985). Inescapable
shock, neurotransmitters, and addiction to trauma: Toward a psychology
of post-traumatic stress. *Biological Psychiatry, 20*, 314–325.

van der Kolk, B., & Saporta, J. (1991). The biological response to psychic
trauma: Mechanisms and treatment of intrusion and numbing. *Anxiety
Research, 4*, 199–212.

Violanti, J. M., Vena, J. E., & Marshall, J. R. (1986). Disease risk and mortality among police officers: New evidence and contributing factors.
Journal of Police Science and Administration, 14, 17–23.

Wegner, D., (1988). Stress and Mental Control,. In S. Fisher & J. Reason
(Eds.), *Handbook of Life, Stress, Cognition, and Health*. New York: John
Wiley & Sons.

ACKNOWLEDGMENTS

THE WRITING OF A BOOK ABOUT THE SOURCES OF INJURY AND death that accompany the peace officer in his or her work is a difficult task, because it puts you face-to-face with the pain caused by the tragedies that occur in law enforcement. To get at the most truthful re-creation of their experiences, I met and spoke with several of the finest people I have ever been honored to meet during my career as a "police shrink." Some were in wheelchairs, some walked with a pronounced limp, and others carried wounds with no visible signs of injury. They offered themselves—and the pain that they have gone through—so that other cops might benefit from the lessons of their experience. I thank them all.

Special thanks go to the members of The Police Survivors, a group of Chicago police officers who suffered serious gunshot wounds or injury from car crashes. They go to other Chicago Police Department (CPD) officers that are similarly harmed and provide support. I thank Chicago senior police officers Steve Tyler, Matthew Koman, Mike Lappe, and Lieutenant Dave Bocian (retired), with special appreciation for the support and help from Detective Patrick Johnson. Pat's letter after he was shot in the back gave me a gift I will cherish always. Each of the above police officers made it back to work despite pain and injury that would have stopped most that attempted it.

Ryan Deuel described the experience of fighting for his life so that other officers would understand the importance of committing themselves to training, practice, and developing skills seriously enough to prepare for that one moment in time when peak performance is the only thing that will save them. He was later awarded the Medal of Valor for his heroism and excellence during a ninety-minute-long gun battle with a barricaded suspect that took the lives of two peace officers. He comes from a family of heroes.

Ryan's father, Lt. Ed Deuel (retired), demonstrated his valor and excellence as a police officer, and his commitment to law enforcement as a teacher and trainer regarding officer-involved shootings. He also taught me much of what I learned about police tactics and the meaning of true friendship.

Captain Rich Wemmer (retired) is a tireless advocate of officer safety, and has contributed thousands of hours teaching peace officers the principles and practices of effective police tactics. He is one of the pioneers of Officer Safety principles and procedures. He often surprised me with the breadth and depth of his knowledge of law enforcement.

I want to acknowledge District Attorney Investigator (retired) Daniel Riter for maintaining his humanity and courage in the face of one of the greatest miscarriages of justice I have ever witnessed. His story appears in chapter 2.

Law enforcement needs strong, positive leaders to achieve its objective of protecting the innocent. I met some who led agencies because of the rank they had; as well as a number who epitomized the traits that give hope for leadership excellence in law enforcement.

An example of this excellence in law enforcement leadership is Chief Ken Corney of the Ventura, California, Police Department. His integrity, his care and support for his employees, and pioneer efforts in training provide optimism for the future of a profession that is constantly asked to do more with fewer resources. I thank Chief Ron DePompa of the Glendale, California, Police Department for his efforts in pioneering mentoring and support programs to assist their employees in achieving success in career and life.

I thank Deputy Chief Scott Whitney for his support in helping to provide tactical decision making and stress exposure management training for the officers of the Oxnard Police Department. While on the subject of Oxnard PD, I thank Sgt. Jack Kujawa for demonstrating the meaning of courage in his return from life-threatening wounds.

The Huntington Beach Police Department's Trauma Response Team has helped to save the careers of scores of peace officers and pioneered a program that gives psychological first aid to fellow officers involved in critical incidents.

I thank the California Narcotics Officers Association for their commitment to education and training for peace officers. Their commitment to training was inspirational. My twenty-one-year relationship with them is a treasure to me.

I thank the peace officers that allowed me to contribute to their health and safety over a thirty-one-year career. You'll never know how many people you have saved.

I thank Gene Gollogly, president of Lantern Books, for giving me the opportunity to write, Wendy Lee, who edited this book, and Kara Davis, who saw it through production.

Finally, I give thanks to my best friend, partner, and wife of forty-three years, Paula Blum. It was difficult for her to deal with the impact that the catastrophes of law enforcement had upon our relationship. When asked recently what the secret was to the longevity of our marriage and love affair, she replied, "I never learned to shoot."

ABOUT THE PUBLISHER

LANTERN BOOKS was founded in 1999 on the principle of living with a greater depth and commitment to the preservation of the natural world. In addition to publishing books on animal advocacy, vegetarianism, religion, and environmentalism, Lantern is dedicated to printing books in the U.S. on recycled paper and saving resources in day-to-day operations. Lantern is honored to be a recipient of the highest standard in environmentally responsible publishing from the Green Press Initiative.

www.lanternbooks.com

Awarded in 2011